COMMON CORE
English Language Arts

in a PLC at Work™

GRADES 3-5

DOUGLAS FISHER
NANCY FREY

Foreword by Rebecca DuFour

A Joint Publication With

INTERNATIONAL
Reading
Association

555 North Morton Street
Bloomington, IN 47404
800.733.6786 (toll free) / 812.336.7700
FAX: 812.336.7790

email: info@solution-tree.com
solution-tree.com

Visit **go.solution-tree.com/commoncore** to download the reproducibles in this book.

Printed in the United States of America

16 15 14 13   4 5

IRA Stock No. 9244

FSC
www.fsc.org
MIX
Paper from
responsible sources
FSC® C011935

Library of Congress Cataloging-in-Publication Data

Fisher, Douglas, 1965-
   Common core English language arts in a PLC at work, grades 3-5 / Douglas Fisher, Nancy Frey.
      p. cm.
   Includes bibliographical references and index.
   ISBN 978-1-936764-19-8 (perfect bound) 1. Language arts (Elementary)--Standards--United States. 2. Language arts (Elementary)--Curricula--United States. 3. Professional learning communities. I. Frey, Nancy, 1959- II. Title.
   LB1576.F442 2013
   372.6--dc23
                              2012031396

Solution Tree
Jeffrey C. Jones, CEO
Edmund M. Ackerman, President

Solution Tree Press
President: Douglas M. Rife
Publisher: Robert D. Clouse
Editorial Director: Lesley Bolton
Managing Production Editor: Caroline Wise
Senior Production Editor: Joan Irwin
Copy Editor: Sarah Payne-Mills
Proofreader: Ashante Thomas
Cover and Text Designer: Jenn Taylor

ACKNOWLEDGMENTS

Solution Tree Press would like to thank the following reviewers:

Deb Cale
Reading/LA/ELL Coordinator
Johnston Community School District
Johnston, Iowa

Luane Genest
Fifth-Grade Teacher
Fairgrounds Elementary School
Nashua, New Hampshire

Angie Kleczewski
Third-Grade Teacher
Dean Elementary School
Brown Deer, Wisconsin

Judith Martin
Interim Director
Sonoma County Office of Education
Santa Rosa, California

Casey Robison
Fourth-Grade Teacher
Farragut Intermediate
Knoxville, Tennessee

Anne Zdrojewski
Literacy Coach
Hidden Valley Elementary School
Charlotte, North Carolina

Visit **go.solution-tree.com/commoncore** to download the reproducibles in this book.

TABLE OF CONTENTS

CHAPTER 3

Implementing the Common Core State Standards for Writing 61

CHAPTER 4

Implementing the Common Core State Standards for Speaking and Listening and for Language 97

CHAPTER 5

Implementing Formative Assessments to Guide Instruction and Intervention 133

ABOUT THE AUTHORS

Douglas Fisher, PhD, is professor of educational leadership at San Diego State University and a teacher leader at Health Sciences High and Middle College. He teaches courses in instructional improvement. As a classroom teacher, Fisher focuses on English language arts instruction. He also serves as the literacy instructional advisor to the Chula Vista Elementary School District.

Fisher received an International Reading Association Celebrate Literacy Award for his work on literacy leadership and was elected to the board of directors in 2012. For his work as codirector of the City Heights Professional Development Schools, Fisher received the Christa McAuliffe award. He was corecipient of the Farmer Award for excellence in writing from the National Council of Teachers of English for the article, "Using Graphic Novels, Anime, and the Internet in an Urban High School," published in the *English Journal*.

Fisher has written numerous articles on reading and literacy, differentiated instruction, and curriculum design. His books include *In a Reading State of Mind, Checking for Understanding, Better Learning Through Structured Teaching*, and *Text Complexity*.

He earned a bachelor's degree in communication, a master's degree in public health education, and a doctoral degree in multicultural education. Fisher completed postdoctoral study at the National Association of State Boards of Education focused on standards-based reforms.

Nancy Frey, PhD, is a professor of literacy in the School of Teacher Education at San Diego State University. Through the university's teacher-credentialing and reading specialist programs, she teaches courses on elementary and secondary reading instruction and literacy in content areas, classroom management, and supporting students with diverse learning needs. Frey also teaches at Health Sciences High and Middle College in San Diego. She was a board member of the California Reading Association and a credentialed special educator, reading specialist, and administrator in California.

Before joining the university faculty, Frey was a public school teacher in Florida. She worked at the state level for the Florida Inclusion Network helping districts design systems for supporting students with disabilities in general education classrooms.

She is the recipient of the 2008 Early Career Achievement Award from the National Reading Conference and the Christa McAuliffe Award for excellence in teacher education from the American Association of State Colleges and Universities. She was corecipient of the Farmer Award for excellence in writing from the National Council of Teachers of English for the article "Using Graphic Novels, Anime, and the Internet in an Urban High School."

Frey is author of *The Formative Assessment Action Plan, Productive Group Work, Teaching Students to Read Like Detectives,* and *Content-Area Conversations.* She has written articles for *The Reading Teacher, Journal of Adolescent and Adult Literacy, English Journal, Voices From the Middle, Middle School Journal, Remedial and Special Education,* and *Educational Leadership.*

To book Douglas Fisher or Nancy Frey for professional development, contact pd@solution-tree.com.

FOREWORD

The publication of *Common Core English Language Arts in a PLC at Work™, Grades 3–5* could not be more timely as educators across the United States are gearing up to make the new standards the foundation of their English language arts (ELA) curriculum, instruction, assessment, intervention, enrichment, and professional development processes. The authors, Douglas Fisher and Nancy Frey, are not only two of the United States' most highly regarded experts in ELA but are also educators who have a deep understanding of the steps needed to bring the Common Core standards to life in our classrooms. Fisher and Frey recognize that if students are going to learn these rigorous skills, concepts, and ways of thinking that are essential to their current and future success, then the educators serving those students must no longer work in traditional isolated classrooms but rather must work as members of collaborative teams in schools and districts that function as professional learning communities (PLCs). As the authors state on page 20:

> In fact, chances are good that you are interested in this book because it promises to link an important change—implementing the Common Core State Standards in English language arts—with a process you already know to be powerful: professional learning communities.

Picture an elementary teacher working in a traditional school. He or she will likely be provided a copy of the Common Core State Standards document, may receive a few hours of training from someone in the district, and then essentially will be left to work in isolation for the rest of the year to interpret, teach, and assess each standard to the best of his or her ability. The degree to which the students assigned into that traditional classroom learn each standard will almost exclusively depend on that teacher's understanding of each standard, how much time and energy he or she is able and willing to devote to the new standards, and finally, his or her ability to teach the standards effectively.

Now imagine a team of teachers working in a school that embraces the PLC at Work process. Team members will be provided a copy of the Common Core ELA document and will work together collaboratively to develop a common understanding of what the standards entail. They will be provided time and support to study and discuss each standard in order to clarify, sequence, pace, and assess the standards in a common way across each grade level. Each team will be provided time to collaborate vertically with teams in the grade levels above and below its own to build a strong scope and sequence and a common language for ELA as students progress from one grade to the next. Leadership at the school and district levels will not only provide each team with the necessary time, support, and ongoing training to engage in this critical collaborative work but also put structures in place and empower staffs to build schoolwide systems of intervention, extension, and enrichment for students—providing time and support for each student to take his or her own learning to the next level.

I am confident this book, written by two respected colleagues, will provide you—my heroes working in schools and districts each day—with ideas, strategies, tools, and resources to help you bring the Common Core English language arts standards to life in your classrooms. The students entrusted to you deserve nothing less.

—Rebecca DuFour

INTRODUCTION

The investment of time and expertise by schools and districts to make the transformation into an effective Professional Learning Community (PLC) at Work is about to pay off once again. The adoption of the Common Core State Standards for English language arts (CCSS ELA) represents a significant change in how the education profession looks at curriculum, instruction, and assessment. In addition, the implications for implementation of the CCSS ELA will have ramifications for years to come. As new research on best practices related to the Common Core State Standards is conducted and disseminated, educators will need to interpret these results and determine how best to put them into practice. The PLC process offers an ideal foundational system for doing so. This process provides the necessary conditions and support to accomplish the work of ensuring continuous improvement. Ongoing professional development is embedded into the process, because teachers work as members of high-performing collaborative teams. Becoming a PLC is a process of reculturing a school; the concept is not just another meeting (DuFour, DuFour, & Eaker, 2008; Frey, Fisher, & Everlove, 2009). Effective districtwide or schoolwide PLCs have the following six characteristics (DuFour et al., 2008; DuFour, DuFour, Eaker, & Many, 2010).

1. **Shared mission, vision, values, and goals all focused on student learning:** The *mission* defines why the organization exists; the *vision* defines what the organization can become in the future; the *values* consist of demonstrated attitudes and behaviors that further the vision; and the *goals* are markers used to determine results and assess progress. A thriving PLC immerses itself in the behaviors necessary to the development of these concepts.

2. **A collaborative culture with a focus on learning:** *Collaboration*, an essential ingredient in the PLC process, enables people to work interdependently to improve teaching and learning.

3. **Collective inquiry into best practice and current reality:** *Collective inquiry* is the process through which PLC educators strive to build shared knowledge about research and what works in their classrooms.

4. **Action orientation:** An *action orientation* is characteristic of successful PLCs that learn by doing and recognize the significance and necessity of actions that engage their members in planning learning tasks, implementing them, and evaluating results.

5. **A commitment to continuous improvement:** *Continuous improvement* is a cyclical process that PLCs use to plan, implement, and check to determine the effectiveness of their efforts to improve teaching and learning.

6. **Results orientation:** *Results* are what count for PLCs; they are the measurable outcomes that reveal the success of the collaborative efforts to improve teaching and learning. Results outweigh intentions.

Visit **www.allthingsplc.info** for a glossary of PLC terms.

These six characteristics must be woven into the fabric of the school; they have to become part of the air that teachers, parents, students, and administrators breathe. In creating this culture, PLCs must reach agreement on fundamental issues, including (DuFour et al., 2008):

- What content students should learn

- What common and coherent assessments to develop and use to determine if students have learned the agreed-on curriculum

- How to respond when students do or don't learn the agreed-on curriculum

To accomplish these three tasks, teachers need adequate time to collaborate with their colleagues. We are not suggesting that scheduling time for teachers to collaborate is easy, but without dedicated time, teams will not develop the collaborative structures needed to support student learning, especially if teachers are going to address the Common Core State Standards in grades 3–5. As part of their collaborative team time, teachers in PLCs engage in inquiry into student learning. The following four critical questions of a PLC highlight and provide a foundation for the work of collaborative planning teams (DuFour et al., 2008).

1. What do we want our students to learn?

2. How will we know when they have learned it?

3. How will we respond when some students don't learn?

4. How will we extend and enrich the learning for students who are already proficient?

Professional Development and Professional Learning Communities

Linda Darling-Hammond (2010) summarizes the research on effective professional development as follows:

> Effective professional development is sustained, ongoing, content-focused, and embedded in professional learning communities where teachers work overtime on problems of practice with other teachers in their subject area or school. Furthermore, it focuses on concrete tasks of teaching, assessment, observation, and reflection, looking at how students learn specific content in particular contexts. . . . It is often useful for teachers to be put in the position of studying the very material that they intend to teach to their own students. (pp. 226–227)

In other words, effective professional development is often the opposite of what most teachers receive—it is sustained and embedded within the work of professional learning communities and focused on the actual tasks of teaching using the material teachers use with students. Professional development practices have moved beyond stand-alone workshops to ones that are tied to a school's chosen area of focus. Through the work of researchers like Bruce Joyce and Beverly Showers (1983) and others, educators began to understand that professional development could be linked to the change process. In particular, the value of an agreed-on focus, the need for continued support after the session, and a plan for measuring success have become expected elements of any school's professional development plan. To succeed as a high-performance school, professional development should be part of a teacher's overall involvement in a learning community.

The link between professional development and school change has been further strengthened through PLCs (Eaker, DuFour, & DuFour, 2002). PLCs recognize that teacher collaboration lies at the heart of learning and change. Collaborative planning teams within PLCs are able to bridge theory to practice as they convene regularly to examine student performance data, discuss student progress, develop and implement curricula, and coach one another through meaningful collaborative work between meetings.

The evidence of PLC effectiveness is mounting. A study of elementary teachers in PLCs identifies a strong statistical correlation between their participation in professional learning communities, their classroom cultures, and their use of formative assessments to advance learning (Birenbaum, Kimron, & Shilton, 2011). Robert Bullough and Steven Baugh (2008) find that the conditions created to foster a schoolwide PLC in turn deepened a school-university partnership. In an analysis of nearly four hundred schools as PLCs, Louise Stoll, Ray Bolam, Agnes McMahon, Mike Wallace, and Sally Thomas (2006) note a positive relationship between student achievement, adoption of innovative practices, and healthy learning communities. In fact, Robert Marzano notes that school and district-level PLCs are "probably the most influential movement with regards to actually changing practices in schools" (DuFour & Marzano, 2011, p. x).

Purpose of This Book

We hope we have made the case, however, briefly, that a PLC at the school or district level is vital to school change. Furthermore, collaborative planning teams functioning within the school's PLC provide embedded professional development that sustains change.

In fact, chances are good that you are interested in this book because it promises to link an important change—implementing the Common Core State Standards in English language arts—with a process you already know to be powerful: professional learning communities. The remainder of this book provides collaborative teacher teams with information about the *what* and the *how* of teaching students to master these standards, including how to develop effective formative assessment and respond when students fail to make progress. We expand the Common Core standards so that you and your team can examine them in detail. You will find that each chapter begins with questions for your team to consider, and we invite you to return to these after you examine the standards to discuss implications for instruction, curriculum, assessment, and intervention.

Organization of This Book

This book has been crafted with your collaborative team in mind. Use it as a workbook—mark it up, dog-ear the pages, highlight passages that resonate, underline the ones that raise a question. In the same way that the Common Core ELA standards focus our collective attention on the practices of close reading and argumentation, we hope to contribute to a similar process for your team. The conversation begins in chapter 1 with an overview of the CCSS and the major shifts in our practices as these relate to informational texts, the role of speaking and listening in learning, the development of academic language and vocabulary, and the importance of argumentation in writing. Later in chapter 1, we explain how the standards are organized, so that the thirty-three-page original document and its three appendices become a bit less bewildering. We also discuss what the standards don't say: about English learners, students with disabilities, and those who struggle with literacy. The National Governors Association Center for Best Practices and Council of Chief State School Officers (NGA & CCSSO), developers of the CCSS, provide some general guidelines for students learning English and those who struggle in school, but these are brief summaries and will likely generate a great deal of additional ideas for implementation over the next several years (for more information visit www.corestandards.org/the-standards for the documents "Application of the Standards for English Language Learners" and "Application to Students With Disabilities"). Importantly, these gaps highlight why PLCs are so important. In the words of the NGA and CCSSO (2010a):

> While the Standards focus on what is most essential, they do not describe all that can or should be taught. A great deal is left to the discretion of teachers and curriculum developers. The aim of the Standards is to articulate the fundamentals, not to set out an exhaustive list or a set of restrictions that limits what can be taught beyond what is specified herein. (p. 6)

Chapters 2, 3, and 4 form the heart of this book because they each focus on a specific *strand* addressed in the CCSS. Reading is the subject of chapter 2: each and every standard is examined as it applies to literary and informational texts, as well as the important reading foundational skills of phonics, word recognition, and fluency that are critical in the development of readers in grades 3–5. Chapter 3 turns the spotlight to the Writing standards and similarly reviews each standard as it applies to the major text types students produce: narrative, informational, and persuasive. In chapter 4, we discuss the two sets of Common Core standards that are integral to what we teach and how students learn—through speaking and listening and by understanding and producing academic language and vocabulary.

Chapter 5 returns to the subject of student consideration in the CCSS, including discussion on using formative assessment processes and summative assessment instruments informatively, and designing and implementing interventions for students who are not performing at expected levels.

Know that this book has been designed with you in mind. All of the research cited is specific to grades 3–5. In addition, we've designed scenarios written from the perspective of teachers and students in grades 3–5 to illuminate the standards.

These scenarios are fictionalized accounts of our personal teaching activities and our collective experience working with teachers across grade levels in schools with diverse populations. We have developed these scenarios as a way to make the ELA standards come alive for you, not just in language arts but also in science, mathematics, and social studies. We want you to personalize this experience as you and your collaborative team plan for implementation of the Common Core for English language arts. To begin this process, we encourage you to reflect on and discuss with your colleagues the following questions.

1. What is the status of collaborative teams at your school? Acknowledging the reality of your school's commitment to an effective PLC process is a critical first step that can establish the future direction for collaborative professional growth. Recall the six characteristics of effective PLCs (pages 1–2) and consider the extent to which your PLC embodies these characteristics. If you want to delve deeper into your school's PLC status, you can explore where your school would place on the PLC continuum: preinitiating, initiating, implementing, developing, or sustaining (DuFour et al., 2010). Visit www.allthingsplc.info and search the Tools & Resources section for helpful PLC reproducibles, such as the PLC continuum reproducible "Laying the Foundation" from *Learning by Doing* (DuFour et al., 2010).

2. How are your students performing? Are there areas of need in terms of curriculum development? Are there areas of need in terms of instruction? Are there areas of need in terms of assessment? These questions address key topics for your PLC to consider as you focus on the current status of your school's language arts programs in relation to the expectations of the Common Core ELA standards. Discussions with your collaborative team will enable you to gain insight into *where you are* and *where you need to go* to support and advance your students' language development.

We've designed this book to guide the conversations that are necessary to fully implement the Common Core State Standards. As such, it should serve as a resource that you return to regularly to consider the ways in which student learning can be improved. The anchor standards and the grade-level expectations are the outcomes expected of us as teachers. *Common Core English Language Arts in a PLC at Work, Grades 3–5* provides the process to get there.

CHAPTER 1

Using Collaborative Teams for English Language Arts

KEY QUESTIONS

- To what extent does your team understand the conceptual shifts represented in the Common Core State Standards for English language arts?

- How often are informational texts used in instruction across the day?

- To what extent do teachers at your school use complex texts?

- Do students routinely discuss and develop texts that feature opinions and evidence?

- To what extent do teachers at your school focus on speaking and listening activities?

- In what ways do teachers at your school develop academic vocabulary and language?

A team of fourth-grade teachers is meeting to discuss the results of a common formative assessment it had recently administered. Teachers had previously agreed on a pacing guide for their unit focused on informational texts and had discussed the various ways that they would teach the unit. Unlike most previous state standards, the Common Core State Standards require an integrated approach to lesson development in which teachers build student competence in multiple standards simultaneously. As an example, the teachers' three-week unit had its primary focus on the Reading Standards for Informational Text at the fourth-grade level (RI.4; NGA & CCSSO, 2010a):

- Refer to details and examples in a text when explaining what the text says explicitly and when drawing inferences from the text. (RI.4.1.)

- Determine the meaning of general academic and domain-specific words or phrases in a text relevant to a fourth-grade topic or subject area. (RI.4.4)

- Describe the overall structure (for example, chronology, comparison, cause and effect, problem and solution) of events, ideas, concepts, or information in a text or part of a text. (RI.4.5)

- Explain how an author uses reasons and evidence to support particular points in a text. (RI.4.8) (p. 12)

Of course, teachers always have to consider the complexity of the text and ensure that students are reading appropriate texts. As part of their common formative assessment, these teachers wanted to determine if students could make inferences from what was explicitly stated in a text and if they could use their knowledge of context clues and word parts to understand vocabulary. The teachers asked students to read a selection about Velcro (see figure 1.1) and respond to a number of questions.

Velcro

For thousands of years, man has walked through fields of weeds and arrived home with burrs stuck to his clothing. It's amazing no one took advantage of the problem until 1948.

George de Mestral, a Swiss engineer, returned from a walk one day in 1948 and found some cockleburs clinging to his cloth jacket. When de Mestral loosened them, he examined one under his microscope. The principle was simple. The cocklebur is a maze of thin strands with burrs (or hooks) on the ends that cling to fabrics or animal fur.

By the accident of the cockleburs sticking to his jacket, de Mestral recognized the potential for a practical new fastener. It took eight years to experiment, develop, and perfect the invention, which consists of two strips of nylon fabric. One strip contains thousands of small hooks. The other strip contains small loops. When the two strips are pressed together, they form a strong bond.

Hook-and-loop fastener is what we call it today. Velcro, the name de Mestral gave his product, is the brand most people in the United States know. It is strong, easily separated, lightweight, durable, and washable; it also comes in a variety of colors and won't jam.

There are thousands of uses for hook-and-loop fasteners—on clothing, shoes, watchbands, or backpacks; around the house or garage; in automobiles, aircraft, parachutes, spacesuits, or space shuttles; to secure blood pressure cuffs and artificial heart chambers. The list is never-ending.

The only bad thing about hook-and-loop fasteners is the competition they give the snap, zipper, button, and shoelace industries!

Source: Adapted from Jones, 1991, p. 68.

Figure 1.1: Sample informational text.

One question on the assessment asked students about the meaning of a word in the selection, "What are *burrs*? How did you know or figure out the word?" The fourth-grade teachers' collaborative discussion about this item centers on students' problem-solving abilities.

Hadley Campbell notes, "Eighty-eight percent of the students got this definition correct. I'm really impressed with that because I thought that burrs would be hard for them."

Agreeing, Ryan Cruise adds, "Yeah, and look, only 15 percent of them said that they knew it. The rest of them said that they figured it out, that it was a plant with parts that were like hooks."

Rene Andre comments, "I think that our students did really well on this, and I'm thinking about the students who thought it was a hook because of the punctuation. I think we might have overgeneralized the lesson on context clues. I'd like to revisit that and remind students that the punctuation does not always give an exact definition. Sometimes, it gives something like an example or analogy."

Later in the discussion, the team notes the students' confusion about the following question: "Why did the author say that 'the only bad thing about hook-and-loop fasteners is the competition for the snap, zipper, button, and shoelace industries'?"

Mr. Cruise starts the conversation saying, "They really didn't get this one. The majority of students focused on the word *bad*. Here's a sample response, 'They are bad because they do not stay closed like a zipper.' As we saw, there are lots and lots of examples of students not understanding the idea of competition for other products and instead thinking that the author thought that Velcro was bad or not as worthy as the other things."

Ms. Campbell asks, "So what do we do about this? Was it something we did that confused them?"

Ms. Andre responds, "I don't think so. I mean, it's not like we taught them something contrary. I'm thinking that we need to do a lot more modeling about inferences. I think that to answer this question, they really have to understand what the author is saying and why. They have to get inside the mind of the author, rather than just focus on the individual words. I'd like to try modeling some more, specifically using inferences when value terms are in the text that might throw off the reader. I'd be willing to find some texts and write some sample modeling lessons, if you think that would help."

Ms. Campbell enthusiastically agrees, adding, "I'm not sure that I would have thought about that. I appreciate our time together and your offer to provide us with resources."

Mr. Cruise adds, "I agree. Thank you so much. I feel like we have a handle on this, or at least a plan. So what else do we see in these data?"

Conversations like this are possible when teachers have the opportunity to work together in collaborative planning teams. To teach the Common Core State Standards well, teachers need to collaborate with their colleagues. In doing so, they can ensure learning for *all* students. It is imperative that collaborative team members work to answer the four critical questions of a PLC as they devote attention to the CCSS (DuFour et al., 2008).

1. What do we want our students to learn?

2. How will we know when they have learned it?

3. How will we respond when some students don't learn?

4. How will we extend and enrich the learning for students who are already proficient?

In other words, teachers need to plan together, look at student work together, identify needs for reteaching together, trust one another, and ask for help when they need it. Figure 1.2 (page 10) provides a tool that we have found useful in helping collaborative

Collaborative Team Meeting Logistics	
Grade:	Date:
Lead teacher or facilitator:	
Teachers in attendance:	

Focus

(Check one.)

    ☐ Curriculum pacing guide

    ☐ Strategy implementation

    ☐ Coaching practice

    ☐ Consensus scoring cycle

        + Common assessment development

        + Item analysis (See Item Analysis Summary.)

Discussion points:	Questions raised:
Objective for the coming week:	Resources needed:
Implementation steps:	

Item Analysis Summary

Assessment tool:
Areas of strength in student work:
Areas of weakness in student work:
Teacher practice: What should be preserved?
Teacher practice: Identify gaps between existing and desired practice.
Teacher practice: What aspects of existing practice pose a barrier to implementing desired practice?
Teacher practice: Identify interventions or unit modifications.
Unanswered questions:

Source: Adapted from Fisher & Frey, 2007a. Reprinted with permission. Learn more about ASCD at www.ascd.org.

Figure 1.2: Collaborative team meeting record.

Visit **go.solution-tree.com/commoncore** for a reproducible version of this figure.

teams work together. As part of their overall PLC work, collaborative teams focus on the four critical questions and begin to build the culture of the school in which student learning drives the discussions teachers and administrators have.

Over time, teams will modify and change the tool to suit their unique needs, but to start, it is likely useful to focus on each aspect of the tool. At the top of the form ("Collaborative Team Meeting Logistics"), teachers record the grade level, the date of the meeting, who was facilitating, and who was in attendance. Given that there are different phases that a collaborative team uses to complete the work, we ask that the team agree on its focus for each of its collaborative meeting times. Importantly, there may be two or more foci during a meeting, and we ask teams to complete different forms for each shift in focus. The reason for this is simple: the team learns to integrate the stages as a habit of interaction when it names each stage each time. It also provides a record that the team can use to review past efforts to improve student achievement. School systems are very good at documenting when things are going wrong and not so good at recording successes. Using a tool like the one in figure 1.2 provides a record of success that team members can review when they need to revisit a successful time in the past.

The remainder of the logistics portion of the form focuses on the discussion that team members have, including the development of pacing guides, teaching strategy implementation, and peer advice and coaching. During some of the meetings, the team will develop common assessments or review the results of an assessment. We recommend that teams use the "Item Analysis Summary" portion when they are discussing assessment results since there are a number of specific decisions to be made in terms of intervention and changes in practice.

Teachers are able to hold these types of conversations because they understand the power of PLCs and the conceptual shifts in the Common Core State Standards for English language arts. They also know the specific standards for their grade level and how these are developed across grades 3–5. In this chapter, we will discuss these major shifts represented in the CCSS, especially their implications for teaching English language arts. In addition, we will highlight what is *not* included in the standards.

The Common Core State Standards

The adoption of the Common Core State Standards for the English language arts extends a trend in U.S. education to collaborate across organizations in order to obtain better learning results. Standards-driven policies and practices have yielded notable results, especially in our collective efforts to articulate purposes and learning outcomes to our stakeholders (Gamoran, 2007). This in turn has led to improved alignment between curriculum, instruction, and assessment. But the years have also exposed weaknesses of this system, many of which are related to the disjointed efforts of individual states trying to put their own standards in motion. No matter how effective the process or product, states simply could not share them with other states, as no standards were held in common. Consequently, states, like Arkansas and Arizona, could not pool human and fiscal resources to develop common materials and assessments.

As standards-based assessments rose to prominence in the 2000s, a mosaic of testing results made it virtually impossible to fairly compare the effectiveness of reform efforts across states. The National Governors Association Center for Best Practices and Council of Chief State School Officers sought to rectify these shortcomings by sponsoring the development of a shared set of standards each state could agree on. Beginning in 2010, state boards of education began adopting these standards in English language arts and mathematics. In 2012, nearly all the states adopted them and began work on determining timelines for implementation, as well as methods for assessment.

In an effort to capitalize on new opportunities for collaboration among states, two assessment consortia are developing standards-based assessments. Both the Partnership for Assessment of Readiness for College and Careers (PARCC) and the Smarter Balanced Assessment Consortium (SBAC) consist of representatives from states working to develop assessments of the standards. Some states belong to both and will eventually determine which instruments they will use. While these efforts are works in progress, common themes are emerging from both consortia. For one, it is likely that a significant part of the tests will be computer based. In addition, it is anticipated that benchmark assessments will play a prominent role in order for schools to be better able to identify students who are falling behind. But perhaps the biggest shift in these assessments has to do with the ELA standards themselves. (Visit www.parcconline.org or www.smarterbalanced.org for more information.) In the next sections, we will outline five major changes to how we view literacy teaching and learning.

Shift One: Focus on Reading and Writing to Inform, Persuade, and Convey Experiences

The Common Core ELA standards reflect a trend in elementary literacy that has been occurring since the 1990s: a deepening appreciation of the importance of informational and persuasive texts in a student's *reading diet*, or the range of reading genre and materials students encounter across the year. (For now, we will focus our discussion on informational texts, with further attention to persuasive texts featured later in this chapter in the section on argumentation.) The reasons for increasing informational text usage are often related to the need to improve content knowledge (Moss, 2005), to meet increased demand in digital environments (Schmar-Dobler, 2003), and even to prevent the so-called *fourth-grade slump* (Chall & Jacobs, 2003), which suggests that student achievement stagnates starting in fourth grade. Perhaps reflective of these efforts, access to and use of informational texts appears to be increasing in elementary school. Jognseong Jeong, Janet Gaffney, and Jin-Oh Choi's (2010) study of second-, third-, and fourth-grade classrooms' informational text usage finds that while use hovers at one minute per day in the second-grade classrooms, it greatly accelerates to sixteen minutes per day in third and fourth grades. However, this is still well short of Barbara Moss's (2005) measure of informational text usage on standardized tests—50 percent at the fourth-grade level.

The National Assessment of Educational Progress (NAEP), sometimes called "the nation's report card," has steadily increased the use of informational text passages on its assessments of fourth-, eighth-, and twelfth-grade students across the United States. In keeping with this initiative, the CCSS ELA recommend an evenly divided reading diet of literary and informational texts by the fourth grade (see table 1.1), gradually increasing

Table 1.1: Grade Distribution of Literary and Informational Passages in the 2009 NAEP Framework

Grade	Literary Texts	Informational Texts
4	50 percent	50 percent
8	45 percent	55 percent
12	30 percent	70 percent

Source: Adapted from NGA & CCSSO, 2010a, p. 5.

in grades 3–5 should no longer be allowed to read narrative text; nothing could be further from the truth. Narrative remains essential as a means of conveying ideas and concepts through story. However, just as a nutritional diet limited to only one or two foods cannot provide sufficient nourishment, neither should we limit the types of texts used (not just stacked on the bookshelves) in the classroom. Furthermore, it is helpful to measure the use of informational text across the school day, not only in the reading and language arts block, in which a greater volume of literary texts are used.

Just as the reading diet of learners needs to be expanded, so does their writing repertoire. A key practice is to link the reading of expository texts with original writing in the same genre, as the link between reading and writing abilities is strong in students (Langer, 1986), and there is an especially strong positive longitudinal effect between grades 2 and 6 (Abbott, Beringer, & Fayol, 2010). In other words, consistent exposure to and use of text genres is positively linked to children's growing ability to write within these same genres. In the same way that narrative texts are used as a springboard for young writers to convey their own experiences, informational texts should be used to teach how one explains and persuades. Students in grades 2 through 6 are not fully aware of audience, especially in recognizing what an unseen reader might need or expect from a text they have written (Bereiter & Scardamalia, 1987).

However, Eliza Beth Littleton (1998) finds that students ages five to nine can be taught to use the oral language rhetorical skills needed to explain and persuade. When purposefully taught, these skills transfer to students' writing ability, and students' capacity to write grows with age and experience.

Similarly, Beverly Cox, Timothy Shanahan, and Margaret Tinzmann (1991) find that advancing reading levels for third and fifth graders' expository writing correlates to more sophisticated control of organizational and rhetorical features. They further note:

> The interesting point in this study is that the more subtle and complex aspects of text knowledge, many of which are experienced primarily in extended, written text . . . or more particularly in exposition (writing more complexly organized hierarchical structures) were only developed by those who were learning to read successfully. (p. 203)

Notably, Victoria Purcell-Gates, Nell Duke, and Joseph Martineau (2007) examine the science reading and writing experiences of second- and third-grade students to identify effective teaching practices. They discover that explicit teaching of informational writing forms (for example, All About Cats) in science has little effect, while immersion in authentic science reading and writing is strongly correlated to writing ability in this genre. Also, authentic reading and writing immersion coupled with explicit instruction is most effective for science procedural writing (for example, How to Freeze Water Into Ice). In both cases, these effects hold regardless of socioeconomic factors, such the parents' educational level.

The ELA standards for grades 3–5 call for a major investment in the time teachers spend instructing students to raise their ability to comprehend informational and persuasive texts. This may require an assessment of where and when students use these types of texts across the school day. Additionally, there is a renewed expectation that students can also write in these genres. Much of the research on expository writing for grades 3–5 students reinforces what many of us already knew: immersion in these texts, when coupled with explicit instruction, can lead to more sophisticated writing (Duke & Roberts, 2010; Moss, 2004).

Shift Two: Focus on Increasing Text Complexity

Closely related to an emphasis on informational texts is "steadily increasing text complexity" (NGA & CCSSO, 2010b, p. 2). This aspect has received considerable attention as educators figure out how to apply a three-part model for determining how complex a reading really is. In addition, U.S. school teams are working to design methods for accessing complex texts among students who struggle to read, English learners, and students with special needs. The CCSS ELA define text complexity as "the inherent difficulty of reading and comprehending a text combined with consideration of reader and task variables; in the Standards, a three-part assessment of text difficulty that pairs qualitative and quantitative measures with reader-task considerations" (NGA & CCSSO, 2010b, p. 43). In other words, it is multidimensional, with attention given to (1) *quantitative measures*, such as readability formulae; (2) *qualitative factors*, such as complexity of ideas, organization, and cohesion; and (3) *reader and task considerations*, such as motivation and task difficulty.

The issue of text complexity raises the case for backward planning, with the outcome being that graduating high school students are sufficiently prepared to tackle the kinds of texts they will encounter as they enter college and careers. While this may initially seem to be a remote goal for teachers in grades 3–5, keeping it in mind is helpful in identifying what texts are useful for students in the intermediate grades.

Appendix B of the Common Core ELA (NGA & CCSSO, 2010c), a useful resource for teachers, includes an extensive list of text exemplars to illustrate this concept of text complexity. These text exemplars should not be misconstrued as a required reading list for a specific grade. To do so would be to ignore the third dimension of identifying complex texts: reader and task considerations. A necessary complication is that text exemplars are arranged somewhat differently across grade bands due to the developmental nature of reading in elementary school. Text exemplars for grades 2–3 are listed together, while a separate list is for use in grades 4–5. An examination of the list of exemplars exposes an important difference between the two: the grades 2–3 list includes stories, poetry, drama, and informational texts that students should read themselves, as well as parallel lists for those that can be used as read-alouds. The grades 4–5 list, on the other hand, does not include a second list for read-alouds. We do not believe that this is an indication that older elementary students should not experience read-alouds; in fact the evidence supporting this instructional practice is strong (Manak, 2011; May, 2011). We interpret this as an indication that interactive read-alouds in grades 4 and 5 are a means for preparing students to comprehend increasingly difficult texts rather than an outcome.

Referenced within the standards document is a *staircase* effect to systematically develop students' capacity for understanding more complex texts (NGA & CCSSO, 2010a). This should be considered at several levels of analysis: within a unit of instruction, throughout a school year, and across multiple grades. That is, the texts a student uses at the beginning of a unit to build background knowledge are more explicit, while those that occur later in a unit to deepen student knowledge are less so. Similarly, the texts students utilize early in a given school year are less complex than those that occur near the end. Additionally, students' capacity and stamina for reading complex texts should build across grade-level bands. For this reason, work concerning text complexity should involve at least two collaborative planning team configurations—as teachers work within as well as across grades 3–5—to articulate a cohesive plan. These horizontal and vertical team collaborations ensure that students experience a cohesive curriculum without gaps or redundancy.

Text complexity poses a major challenge for educators in grades 3–5 as students transition to classroom environments that increasingly rely on texts as a major source of learning. Defining what makes a text complex requires analyzing qualitative factors and quantitative measures, while also considering the characteristics of the reader and the demands of the related task. In addition, the CCSS encourage teachers to look across units, the school year, and grade bands to build a purposeful plan to staircase student capacity for complex texts.

Shift Three: Focus on Speaking and Listening

While oral language development is widely regarded as a key feature of early elementary education, in practice this is more often regarded as being of less importance in grades 3–5, except for students with identified language learning needs. Perhaps this is due to more text-based instruction or to larger class sizes. Whatever the specific reason, there is a noticeable decline in the amount of meaningful discussion that occurs in classrooms after the primary grades. Robert Pianta et al. (2007), in observations of 2,500 elementary classrooms, find that fifth-grade teachers spend less than 7 percent of the school day instructing students for analysis and inference, in contrast to nearly 32 percent devoted to basic skills, 18 percent for managerial instructions, and 17 percent for transitions. Notably, these findings are statistically similar as well in third- and first-grade classrooms. It is difficult to see how students can develop critical speaking and listening skills when a large part of their school day involves listening to low-level directions.

The CCSS place a strong emphasis on speaking and listening in the primary grades. Furthermore, NGA and CCSSO state:

> A meta-analysis by Sticht and James (1984) indicates that the importance of oral language extends well beyond the earliest grades. . . . Sticht and James found evidence strongly suggesting that children's listening comprehension outpaces reading comprehension until the middle school years (grades 6–8). (p. 26).

Speaking and listening skills have a concomitant relationship with reading and writing development. To observe this effect, Virginia Berninger and Robert Abbott (2010) examine two cohorts of students from elementary into middle school, measuring their listening comprehension, speaking expression, reading comprehension, and writing comprehension in grades 1, 3, 5, and 7. They note students' relative strengths and weaknesses vary considerably across the years, supporting the assertion that these language modalities are not fixed but are influenced considerably by experiences and education. They note:

> Some [people] still believe that children learn oral language before they come to school and that the purpose of schooling is to teach written language. . . . When the four separate language systems are well integrated and synchronized, language may be experienced as a unitary construct, much as rain is experienced as unitary wetness rather than as isolated drops. (p. 649)

Berninger and Abbott (2010) advocate for a view of "comprehension and expression via language by ear, mouth, hand, and eye" (p. 635), weaving language experiences into as many instructional events as possible.

The Common Core ELA standards for grades 3–5 call for teachers to nest speaking and listening within the context of literacy instruction. Importantly, these performance-based standards include delivering and listening to the presentations of other students and exchanging information and ideas featured in these performance events. Speaking and listening also extend to a variety of instructional arrangements, especially small-group interactions across content areas. Students are encouraged to collaborate with one another and communicate in formal and informal settings; like shifts one and two, they should not be bound exclusively to the reading and language arts block and should be integrated across the school day.

Shift Four: Focus on Text-Based Evidence for Argumentation

A fourth shift concerns the development of argumentation skills. This is unfamiliar to many elementary teachers who typically have experience at rhetorical reading and writing only as college students themselves. Perhaps they recall formal argumentation in writing, such as Stephen Toulmin's (1958) model of argumentation.

- **Claim:** The position being argued; for example, "Our family should get a dog."

- **Grounds:** The reasons given for the claim; answers the question, "What's the proof?" For example, "Dogs have been bred for thousands of years to be good companions and to provide security to their owners."

- **Warrant:** The more formal reasoning or principle that serves as the underpinning for the claim; this links the claim to the grounds such as, "Many families choose a dog for a pet for these reasons."

- **Backing:** The justification for the warrant; for example, "The Humane Society of the United States says that there are seventy-eight million pet dogs, and 39 percent of all households have at least one dog."

- **Rebuttal:** The counterclaim an opponent might assert; such as, "Some parents might worry that they will need to do all the care, but I promise to walk the dog every day."

- **Qualification:** The limits to the claim; for example, "I know I will need help in the beginning because I don't have a lot of experience with dogs. I know I will need to read more about pet care to get really good at it."

Toulmin's (1958) model of argumentation is meant only to illustrate that grades 3–5 students are developmentally capable of laying out a simple argument and supporting it with evidence. While we don't advocate for teaching formal argumentation as Toulmin describes it, the foundations of rational thought are completely within the scope of what students in middle childhood can do. Scott Beers and William Nagy (2011) call this type of thinking *discursive literacy* and consider this a second step for young writers after they have mastered the *linguistic literacy* taught in the primary grades. Indeed, we regularly teach some aspects already: detecting the differences between fact and opinion, recognizing advertising techniques, and even examining propaganda, editorial cartoons, and letters to the editor. Two elements are often missing, however: students rarely engage in formal writing of persuasive essays, and they are seldom required to cite evidence from texts to support their claims (Bransford, Brown, & Cocking, 2000; Davidson, 2011; Leithwood, McAdie, Bascia, & Rodrigue, 2006).

Argumentation as a formal process isn't present in the Common Core ELA until grades 6–12. However, the foundation for it is built in the elementary years through opinion. Importantly, *opinion* doesn't refer to the general definition of the word—after all, everybody has opinions about something—but rather about the academic expectations of opinion. These expectations include stating one's opinion, supporting opinion through evidence and example, and anticipating and addressing opposing opinions. In elementary school, this process is demonstrated through persuasive writing.

Although persuasive writing has been featured in most states' content frameworks, it is rarely put into practice in a consistent way (Moore & MacArthur, 2012). A national survey of teachers in grades 4–6 finds that nearly 80 percent of participating teachers assign persuasive writing *never at all* (8.25 percent) or *several times a year, but less than monthly* (71.13 percent) (Gilbert & Graham, 2010). Students do not write often enough in school. The amount of writing alone is inadequate for them to become more skilled at writing persuasively. Additionally, this may have instructional implications. Writing is more than just assigning; writing skills must be taught as well. Beers and Nagy (2011) note that the writing development of more than one hundred third graders for five years—through seventh grade—in four genres (narrative, descriptive, compare and contrast, and persuasive) progressed slowly over the course of the study, but was especially slow for persuasive writing. Noting that the syntactic demand of persuasive writing is challenging for young writers, Beers and Nagy (2011) state:

> Children face two steep learning curves in their attempts to develop as writers: they must acquire academic vocabulary and the ability to use increasingly complex syntactic forms, and they also must learn to use these newly-acquired linguistic tools correctly in a variety of different genres. (p. 185)

Persuasive writing requires the use of subordinate clauses, and students inexperienced in using subordinate clauses are unable to adequately develop more sophisticated persuasive-writing abilities. (For example, "Because dogs make excellent watch dogs, families feel more protected.")

A second characteristic of persuasion and argumentation is the ability to cite evidence to support one's claims. The use of evidence is at the heart of science instruction. The National Science Education Association standards (National Research Council, 1996) require elementary science students to use evidence for argumentation in science discussion and writing. Argumentation skills, like persuasion skills, can be taught. However, they require purposeful instruction. For example, Katherine McNeill (2011) chronicles the development of fifth-grade science students' growing ability to use evidence and argumentation in their science writing. The teacher consistently taught about science discourse in discussions and writings using claims, evidence, and reasoning (backing). At the beginning of the school year, most of the students in the study wrote using the limited language of general descriptions, while only 28 percent wrote using argumentation. By the end of the school year, and with instruction coupled with authentic purposes, 100 percent of the students were able to use argumentation in science. These findings further support Purcell-Gates, Duke, and Martineau's (2007) study, which shows that third-grade students' science writing improved significantly when authentic purposes for reading and writing were coupled with explicit instruction on the techniques needed to do so. (See chapter 3 for descriptions of writing instruction practices.) Science is an ideal environment for introducing the concept of argumentation, but these skills can and should be reinforced throughout the school day.

The CCSS ELA encourage the purposeful teaching of developmentally appropriate elements of opinion, argumentation, and persuasion to expand students' breadth and depth of writing. These rhetorical skills become increasingly essential as students progress through middle and high school, with the seeds of logic sown in the elementary years. Students gain these skills through reading and writing in small-group discussions and classroom discourse.

Shift Five: Focus on Academic Vocabulary and Language

A final shift in the Common Core standards concerns the development of academic vocabulary and language. As with the other major conceptual changes, this shift's intent is to foster disciplinary links in order to build learning. This approach acknowledges that vocabulary should not be seen as an isolated list of words but rather as labels that we use as a proxy for conceptual understandings. In fact, the language of the standards illuminates this idea. The CCSS note the use of "general academic and domain-specific words and phrases sufficient for reading, writing, speaking, and listening" (NGA & CCSSO, 2010a, p. 25). This underscores two key points: (1) academic vocabulary and language entails the use of a broad range of terms—*lexical dexterity*—and (2) vocabulary development extends beyond teaching decontextualized words (NGA & CCSSO, 2010b).

Much of the research underpinning this view of academic vocabulary and language comes from the work of Isabel Beck, Margaret McKeown, and Linda Kucan (2008), whose familiar three-tier model categorizes words and their instruction.

1. **Tier one:** These words are used in everyday speech, are in the vocabulary of most native speakers, and are taught only in the primary grades. However, students who need more language support, such as English learners, will need instruction beyond the first years of schooling. Examples of tier one words include *clock*, *happy*, and *baby* (Beck, McKeown, & Kucan, 2002).

2. **Tier two:** These words (called *general academic words and phrases* in the CCSS) appear more often in texts than in verbal exchanges. For instance, *maintain*, *merchant*, and *benevolent* are examples of tier two words for fourth-grade students (Beck et al., 2002). In addition, tier two words are used in many kinds of texts, not just those that are found within a specific discipline. These words need to be explicitly taught throughout the school years.

3. **Tier three:** These words (called *domain-specific words and phrases* in the CCSS) are closely associated with a specific content and also require specific instruction. Examples of such words and phrases at fourth grade include *magnetic field*, *decimals*, and *prime meridian*.

While teachers often give tier three words and phrases quite a bit of attention, tier two words are more often overlooked. After all, domain-specific words and phrases are closely tied to a discipline and a unit of instruction, and attention is therefore focused on knowing both the definition of the word and its associated concepts. But by overlooking tier two words in instruction, students can face more difficulty reading complex texts because these words "are not unique to a particular discipline . . . are far less well defined by contextual clues . . . and far less likely to be defined explicitly within a text" (NGA & CCSSO, 2010b, p. 33). For example, knowing that a character *sauntered* rather than *ran* alerts the reader to the character's mood and intent. A *benevolent* leader enlightens a reader to the intentions of an expeditionary team. But unless attention is also provided for these words, readers of complex texts are not able to comprehend at a deeper level. Similarly, students will not use sophisticated terms in their expressive language.

Therefore, an important shift in the Common Core standards concerns the importance of using academic language and vocabulary throughout the school day. Special attention should be given to the types of academic language students require in order to express themselves and to understand the writings of others. Furthermore, the rush to profile domain-specific words and phrases can overshadow the importance of general academic vocabulary that students encounter in many kinds of texts. The investment in academic vocabulary and language is well worth it, as vocabulary knowledge is a robust predictor of reading comprehension through eighth grade (Yovanoff, Duesbery, & Alonzo, 2005).

Purposes and Organization of the CCSS ELA

In the previous section, we highlighted five major shifts in the way we look at the literacy development of grades 3–5 students across the school day. As noted previously, a primary purpose of the CCSS is to prepare students for eventual college or career choices. All schools aspire to successfully prepare students for the future; however, some argue that starting this in high school is too late for some students (National Education Goals Panel, 1998). However, this doesn't mean that elementary students must start making plans for their adult lives. But insufficient literacy skills do limit one's choices in employment, careers, and postsecondary education. By spotlighting the importance of literacy development across grades K–12, we hope to collectively consider how 21st century instruction factors into students' lives long after they have left our classrooms.

The CCSS spotlight college and career readiness with *anchor standards*. Anchor standards are the threads that tie the grade-level standards together, whether in kindergarten or senior year. Anchor standards frame each language arts strand: Reading, Writing, Speaking and Listening, and Language. Figure 1.3 explains the different elements of the Common Core State Standards for English language arts.

In the next three chapters, we utilize the anchor standards as a means for fostering the work of collaborative planning teams. The following principles for college and career readiness shape these anchor standards and describe the growing capabilities of learners as they progress through school. To be college and career ready, students must do the following.

- **Demonstrate independence:** Students must comprehend complex texts in all content areas, participate as speakers and listeners in academic discussions and presentations, direct their own learning, and utilize resources.

Strands are the categories for English language arts in K–5 and 6–12: Reading, Writing, Speaking and Listening, and Language. Additionally, literacy in history and social studies, science, and technical subjects in grades 6–12 focuses on two strands—Reading and Writing.

College and career readiness (CCR) anchor standards define general, cross-disciplinary expectations for reading, writing, speaking and listening, and language. These anchor standards are designated by strand and standard number; for example, R.CCR.6 signifies reading strand (R), anchor standard (CCR), and standard number (six). This standard is from the domain Craft and Structure, which has three standards numbered four, five, and six. The anchor standards are numbered consecutively, one through ten, in the domains.

Domains define categories of CCR anchor standards for each of the strands in the CCSS ELA—Reading, Writing, Speaking and Listening, and Language. For example, four domains are defined for the Writing strand: Text Types and Purposes (standards one, two, and three), Production and Distribution of Writing (standards four, five, and six), Research to Build and Present Knowledge (standards seven, eight, and nine), and Range of Writing (standard ten).

Grade-specific standards define what students should understand and be able to do. The grade-specific standards parallel the CCR anchor standards by translating the broader CCR statements into grade-appropriate end-of-year expectations.

Grade-specific standards are designated by strand, anchor standard, grade level, and standard number; for example, RL.K.1 signifies Reading Standards for Literature (RL), kindergarten level (K), standard one in the domain Key Ideas and Details.

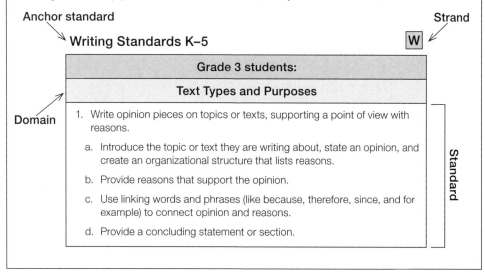

Source: Adapted from NGA & CCSSO, 2010a, p. 20.

Figure 1.3: How to read the CCSS ELA.

- **Build strong content knowledge across all subjects and disciplines:** Cross-discipline knowledge is important for students' writing and discussions. In addition, students should engage in the research and study skills needed to build their content knowledge.

- **Respond to the varying demands of audience, task, purpose, and discipline:** College- and career-ready students communicate in speaking and writing with a range of audiences and are knowledgeable about the variances of discipline-specific evidence.

- **Comprehend as well as critique:** Students learn this skill as they read and listen to others. They are able to ask questions, evaluate information, and discern reasonableness.

- **Value evidence:** Students should provide evidence in their own oral and written discourse and expect others to furnish evidence.

- **Use technology and digital media strategically and capably:** As they integrate online and offline resources, students should use critical-thinking and communication skills within their digital lives.

- **Understand other perspectives and cultures:** In order to better communicate with and learn from and alongside people, students should understand a wide range of cultural and experiential backgrounds.

The principles and assumptions that guided development of the anchor standards provide a framework for understanding them and their function in girding the grade-level standards. While the CCSS map the territory for literacy development, they do not pretend to describe every aspect of teaching and learning.

What Is Not Covered in the Standards

Keep in mind that the standards themselves are end-point results. It has been left to educators, instructional leaders, collaborative planning teams, and curriculum developers to design the ways to get there. The CCSS state, "The Standards define what all students are expected to know and be able to do, not how teachers should teach" (NGA & CCSSO, 2010a, p. 6). This is intentional, as it is essential for educators at the local, state, and national levels to engage in dialogue about essential topics related to content and scope, intervention methods and materials, and supports and expectations for English learners, students with special needs, and students who struggle.

The Content and Scope

The Common Core ELA standards describe essential outcomes but do not address all aspects of learning, or even disciplines, that are important for learners. The authors use play as an example, acknowledging that it is critical in the learning lives of young children but is not featured in the standards themselves (NGA & CCSSO, 2010a). Even within the scope of English language arts, not all aspects are featured. For instance, handwriting is not mentioned, even though every elementary teacher devotes time to this endeavor. Consequently, some states have supplemented the standards with additional content. For example, California added 15 percent of content to the CCSS, such as handwriting, presentation, and recitation standards in grades 3–5 (California Department of Education, n.d.; Sacramento County Office of Education, 2012). The Common Core State Standards are intended to guide the development of formative and summative assessments. It is important for states to cap their additions to ensure they do not undermine this design and make it impossible to develop meaningful assessments that can be used across states. This process will ensure that assessment results based on the CCSS will allow for comparisons of student performance across states. PARCC and SBAC, the two consortia developing standards-based assessments, consist of representatives from states that provide additional opportunities for collaboration among states. Teachers should check their state's department of education website to determine any content that's been added to the CCSS.

Intervention Methods and Materials

The standards should be viewed as end-of-grade expectations, but they do not in any way describe either the approaches for intervention or the materials used to accompany them. In every school, some students are performing well below grade-level expectations, and others are currently benefitting from a response to intervention (RTI) approach to learning. RTI involves identifying whether, and to what extent, a struggling student is responding positively to intervention that has been designed to meet the individual learner's needs. His or her responsiveness (or unresponsiveness) to intervention is determined through dynamic, ongoing assessment that monitors student progress and shapes modifications to the assessment plan. The CCSS ELA do not discuss RTI; however, we will explore this topic in chapter 5.

Supports and Expectations for English Learners

The NGA and CCSSO include people knowledgeable about issues related to English learners. NGA and CCSSO acknowledge that students acquiring English require supports and that these supports should be carefully designed to meet the needs of these students (see "Application of Common Core State Standards for English Language Learners," www.corestandards.org/assets/application-for-english-learners.pdf). They caution, however, that accommodations should not result in a reduction of expectations for fear that the trajectory of these students' educational progress will be severely compromised.

Supports and Expectations for Students With Special Needs

Similarly, the CCSS do not define supports for students with special needs beyond assistive technologies such as Braille, screen-reader technologies, sign language, and so on. Use of such devices is determined through an individual education program (IEP) and supersedes educational standards. These devices and approaches are more commonly used for students with sensory or motor disabilities, or in some cases, for those with mild disabilities that involve reading and learning (see "Application to Students With Disabilities," www.corestandards.org/assets/application-to-students-with-disabilities.pdf). What has not been determined is how these supports and expectations might be adapted for students with more significant cognitive and intellectual delays and disabilities. It is likely that development of these systems will continue as general and special educators collaborate. Participation and access are priorities, and the CCSS language mirrors that used in the Individuals With Disabilities Education Improvement Act of 2004 (http://idea.ed.gov): "The Standards should also be read as allowing for the widest possible range of students to participate fully from the outset and as permitting appropriate accommodations to ensure maximum participation of students with special education needs" (NGA & CCSSO, 2010a, p. 6).

Support and Expectations for Students Who Struggle

The Common Core State Standards do not provide specific advice about supporting students who struggle with school. Instead, there is a recognition that expectations are often reduced and students fail to reach high levels of achievement. Support for students who struggle with school should be part of the ongoing conversations within collaborative planning teams. As Richard DuFour, Rebecca DuFour, and Robert Eaker (2008) note, collaborative teams should discuss what to do when students fail to achieve the expected learning targets. During discussions, team members can identify additional instructional interventions to close the gap between students who mastered the content and those who did not. This may involve reteaching content through guided instruction or targeting students for RTI efforts (Fisher & Frey, 2010). A pyramid of RTI that provides teams with systems for intervention can be helpful (Buffum, Mattos, & Weber, 2008). Additionally, in this book we will focus on quality teaching for all students and encourage the development of collaborative planning teams to monitor and adapt instruction to ensure learning for all students. This systematic approach to students who struggle in school has a better potential to result in positive outcomes than reducing expectations or preventing students from accessing high-quality instruction aligned with the Common Core State Standards. That's not to say that teachers should avoid scaffolding or support. As we will discuss in each of the teaching scenarios in this book, teaching Common Core ELA well requires a deep understanding of the content as well as skills in responding to students' understanding and misunderstanding.

Conclusion

The Common Core State Standards for English language arts present grades 3–5 educators with challenges as well as opportunities. The shifts in our ways of thinking about literacy development are considerable and require us to collectively look at our own practices and plan collaboratively with our colleagues. These expectations can pose a major roadblock for schools that do not have a forum for conducting this important work. It is not the kind of work that can be accomplished in a few workshops and some follow-up meetings. Determining how these changes will be implemented, as well as identifying the effective practices that have already proven to be successful, will require focused and sustained attention as educators together develop curriculum, design formative assessments, and interpret results. Collaborative teams within a professional learning community are an ideal forum for accomplishing this work. Indeed, the major shifts described in this chapter parallel the characteristics of successful professional learning communities: they emphasize collaboration and communication across disciplines and grade levels, and they reward those who seek to deepen their understanding of their professional practice.

CHAPTER 2

Implementing the Common Core State Standards for Reading

KEY QUESTIONS

- To what extent does your team understand the Reading standards: What is familiar? What is new? What may be challenging for students? What may be challenging for teachers?

- Examine current texts being used in grades 3–5 and assess them quantitatively and qualitatively and for reader and task demands. Which ones work? Which ones should be used in another grade or eliminated all together?

- How do grades 3–5 teachers at your school extend the foundational skills of reading that are taught in grades K–2?

Consuelo Martinez's third-grade students are exploring the world around them without ever leaving their classroom. They have been reading *If the World Were a Village: A Book About the World's People* (Smith, 2002) to understand the diverse makeup of the world's cultures and to see their place within them. The book's premise is that the descriptive statistics of the world's population can be understood as an imaginary village of one hundred people. Ms. Martinez is using this informational text within the students' mathematics class.

"It is giving me a great way to introduce fractions before they even realize it. I want them to get the number sense of a whole and its parts, and this text is providing me a way to discuss the concept of proportions," she explains to her collaborative team.

In addition to building mathematical knowledge, the class is also learning how to approach an informational text that is arranged in an uncommon fashion.

"Many of the informational texts students read are meant to be consumed from beginning to end, while others are reference books that you use to look up something," Ms. Martinez explains. "Our grade level also wants to give students experience at reading informational texts that are designed to dip in and out of," she says.

On the first day of this unit, the class reads and discusses the purpose of the book and reads the opening passage, titled "Welcome to the Global Village" (Smith, 2002, p. 7). They also consult the endnotes on how the calculations were made. She says, "By examining this, we were able to draw some conclusions about the credibility of the author and accuracy of the statistics in the book."

For a few weeks, the class reads a different self-contained page each day and discusses the text at length. "I start each lesson by having them examine the table of contents to reinforce the idea that this can be read in any order," she says. They began by looking at easier concepts, such as distributions of age and languages, and moved on to nationalities. "We placed sticky notes with facts we've gleaned on our classroom map of the world," she adds. "We're also evaluating what the author means when he uses mathematical estimation terms like *more than half, nearly, most, divided equally, at least, slightly less than,* and *average,* as well as fractional language like *one-fifth* and *doubled.* It's amazing to see how much literacy, social studies, and math instruction I can capitalize on using just this one text," Ms. Martinez remarks. Understanding the author's calculations and the vocabulary terms helps students to meet standards in the grades 3–5 mathematics domains Operations and Algebraic Thinking and Measurement and Data. Furthermore, the activity calls on students to use two of the CCSS Mathematical Practices: Mathematical Practice 2, Reason abstractly and quantitatively, and Mathematical Practice 3, Construct viable arguments and critique the reasoning of others (see NGA & CCSSO, 2010e).

A Collaborative Planning Team in Action

Before delving into the main purpose of this chapter, which is to examine the Common Core State Standards for reading in grades 3–5, we want to comment on Ms. Martinez's curricular decisions and the contributions of her collaborative planning team toward those decisions.

Working together, Ms. Martinez and her collaborative team developed a consistent and coherent approach for planning the instructional unit by taking the following actions:

- Examining the text exemplars list in appendix B of the CCSS (NGA & CCSSO, 2010c) to gain a sense of the text complexity appropriate for third-grade students

- Identifying texts they currently use to teach students how to compare and contrast

- Creating a list identifying a range of informational texts and literature readings that represented a progression of complexity throughout the school year

- Matching identified texts to concepts and content to be taught in third grade, including in mathematics, social studies, science, and the visual and performing arts

- Developing lessons to be delivered and common formative assessments to be administered

- Discussing findings with one another during their weekly team meetings

- Developing a classroom observation schedule so they could spend time in one another's classrooms

In other words, Ms. Martinez didn't work alone to develop a unit using informational text in her mathematics class. She relied on the collective strengths of her collaborative planning team to develop this unit and analyze student outcomes. However, before the team could engage in these actions, members had to analyze the Common Core ELA standards and compare these to their existing curriculum and instruction. They used four questions to guide their analysis.

1. What is familiar in the CCSS at each grade level?

2. What appears to be new based on prior standards?

3. What may be challenging for students?

4. What may be challenging for teachers?

This initial conversation allowed this teacher team to begin an analysis of its current status in curriculum and instruction. Importantly, teachers also included student learning from the outset. Based on its initial work, the team was able to identify areas of need regarding professional development and materials acquisition and set the stage for later decisions regarding curriculum development, data analysis, intervention, and collaborative observations. A copy of this initial tool Ms. Martinez's collaborative team used is shown in figure 2.1 (page 30). Visit **go.solution-tree.com/commoncore** for an online-only reproducible of figure 2.1, which your collaborative team can use to analyze other reading standards.

Anchor Standards for Reading

The Common Core English language arts standards are organized across four *strands*: Reading, Writing, Speaking and Listening, and Language. As discussed in chapter 1, a set of K–12 anchor standards for college and career readiness frames each strand. These anchor standards articulate the overarching goals that shape the grade-specific standards and are designed to create commonality across elementary, middle, and high school. "Students advancing through the grades are expected to meet each year's grade-specific standards and retain or further develop skills and understandings mastered in preceding grades" (NGA & CCSSO, 2010a, p. 11). This structure can reduce the *silo effect* that can creep into education in which teachers work in isolation from their peers and curriculum is not coordinated. By viewing education across grade bands and buildings, we can begin to mirror more closely the experiences of our students and their families. The anchor standards are an attempt to foster communication across and within educational systems.

There are ten K–5 anchor standards for reading organized into the following four domains (NGA & CCSSO, 2010a, p. 10).

1. Key Ideas and Details

2. Craft and Structure

3. Integration of Knowledge and Ideas

4. Range of Reading and Level of Text Complexity

Reading anchor standard five (R.CCR.5): Analyze the structure of texts, including how specific sentences, paragraphs, and larger portions of the text (a section, chapter, scene, or stanza) relate to each other and the whole.

CCSS grade band: Grades 3–5

CCSS strand: Reading Standards for Informational Text (RI)

Anchor standard domain: Craft and Structure

Grade-Level Standard	What Is Familiar?	What Is New?	What May Be Challenging for Students?	What May Be Challenging for Teachers?
Grade 3 **RI.3.5:** Use text features and search tools (like key words, sidebars, and hyperlinks) to locate information relevant to a given topic efficiently.				
Grade 4 **RI.4.5:** Describe the overall structure (such as chronology, comparison, cause and effect, problem and solution) of events, ideas, concepts, or information in a text or part of a text.				
Grade 5 **RI.5.5:** Compare and contrast the overall structure (such as chronology, comparison, cause and effect, problem and solution) of events, ideas, concepts, or information in two or more texts.				

Source: Adapted from NGA & CCSSO, 2010a, pp. 10 and 14.

Figure 2.1: Guiding questions for grade-by-grade analysis of the Reading standards.

Visit **go.solution-tree.com/commoncore** for a reproducible version of this figure.

These anchor standards are directly tied to two parts within the Reading strand at grades K–12: Literature and Informational Text. A third part, Foundational Skills, is specific to K–5 only; it is the only one that does not have a set of anchor standards. We will examine each of these in this chapter, after first discussing the anchor standards in more detail.

Key Ideas and Details

The first three anchor standards describe the explicit and implicit comprehension of readers as they glean the purposes and main points of the text. In addition, the domain emphasizes the importance of being able to follow plot, character development, and themes, all necessary for literary analysis.

1. Read closely to determine what the text says explicitly and to make logical inferences from it; cite specific textual evidence when writing or speaking to support conclusions drawn from the text. (R.CCR.1)

2. Determine central ideas or themes of a text and analyze their development; summarize the key supporting details and ideas. (R.CCR.2)

3. Analyze how and why individuals, events, and ideas develop and interact over the course of a text. (R.CCR.3) (NGA & CCSSO, 2010a, p. 10)

Craft and Structure

The three anchor standards in this domain discuss the reader's ability to analyze texts at the micro and macro levels. Readers should attend to the author's craft in how he or she purposefully uses word choice, literary techniques, and organizational structures to shape the text; a character's voice and experiences; or the interaction between the choice of genre and the information shared.

4. Interpret words and phrases as they are used in a text, including determining technical, connotative, and figurative meanings, and analyze how specific word choices shape meaning or tone. (R.CCR.4)

5. Analyze the structure of texts, including how specific sentences, paragraphs, and larger portions of the text (e.g., a section, chapter, scene, or stanza) relate to each other and the whole. (R.CCR.5)

6. Assess how point of view or purpose shapes the content and style of a text. (R.CCR.6) (NGA & CCSSO, 2010a, p. 10)

Integration of Knowledge and Ideas

In this domain, anchor standards seven through nine are dedicated to the content within and across texts, in print, and in digital environments. Anchor standard seven (R.CCR.7) is also closely tied to the Writing anchor standard domain Research to Build and Present Knowledge (see NGA & CCSSO, 2010a, p. 21), as well as the Speaking and Listening anchor standard domain Comprehension and Collaboration (see NGA & CCSSO, 2010a, p. 24). Anchor standard eight (R.CCR.8) on argumentation is not addressed in the Literature part as it is not applicable to these text types.

7. Integrate and evaluate content presented in diverse media and formats, including visually and quantitatively, as well as in words. (R.CCR.7)

8. Delineate and evaluate the argument and specific claims in a text, including the validity of the reasoning as well as the relevance and sufficiency of the evidence. (R.CCR.8)

9. Analyze how two or more texts address similar themes or topics in order to build knowledge or to compare the approaches the authors take. (R.CCR.9) (NGA & CCSSO, 2010a, p. 10)

Range of Reading and Level of Text Complexity

This domain with the tenth and final anchor standard for reading has arguably been the predominant topic of discussion about the CCSS ELA.

10. Read and comprehend complex literary and informational texts independently and proficiently. (R.CCR.10) (NGA & CCSSO, 2010a, p. 10)

The Common Core ELA and its appendices devote a considerable amount of space to this standard, noting that students' use of complex texts has diminished since at least the 1970s, while texts used in college and the workplace have not (Chall, Conard, & Harris, 1977; Hayes, Wolfer, & Wolfe, 1996; as cited in NGA & CCSSO, 2010b). The CCSS advocate for a staircase approach to systematically raising reading comprehension and critical thinking through the purposeful use of complex texts that require students to stretch their cognitive and metacognitive abilities (NGA & CCSSO, 2010a). For students who struggle with reading, this means that they must be taught with complex texts and asked to read increasingly complex texts across the year. However, it is important to note that the text alone should not be the only scaffold; instruction is critical for these students to progress and accelerate.

Text complexity is defined across three dimensions: (1) quantitative measures, (2) qualitative factors, and (3) reader and task considerations. Quantitative measures, using a mixture of word length, sentence length, and syllables, are familiar to elementary educators. In addition, many readability formulae calculate the number of difficult words that appear in a text by comparing these to grade-level lists. Examples of quantitative measures include the Fry Readability Formula, Dale-Chall Readability Formula, and Flesch-Kincaid Grade-Level Index (see Fisher, Frey, & Lapp, 2012), as well as commercial ones such as ATOS (used by Accelerated Reader), Source Rater (Educational Testing Service), Pearson Reading Maturity Scale (Pearson Education), Degrees of Reading Power (Questar), and Lexile (MetaMetrics). Table 2.1 compares these readability scales. Published quantitative reading scores can provide a platform for collaborative teams to begin to examine which texts to use with their students.

The Lexile measures used in the CCSS have been revised; consequently, the measures in table 2.1 differ from those provided in appendix A of the Common Core for ELA (see NGA & CCSSO, 2010b, p. 8). For example, the original range for the 2–3 grade band was 450–720L compared to the revised range of 420–820L. Lexile measures are based on word frequency (semantic difficulty) and sentence length (syntactic complexity), both of which have been shown to be effective predictors of text difficulty (Lennon & Burdick, 2004).

Table 2.1: Text Complexity Ranges Within Grade Bands

Grade Band	Revised CCSS 2011	Accelerated Reader	Degrees of Reading Power	Flesch-Kincaid	Source Rater	Reading Maturity Scale
K–1	n/a	n/a	n/a	n/a	n/a	n/a
2–3	420–820	2.75–5.14	42–54	1.98–5.34	0.05–2.48	3.53–6.13
4–5	740–1010	4.97–7.03	52–60	4.51–7.73	0.84–5.75	5.42–7.92
6–8	925–1185	7.00–9.98	57–67	6.51–10.34	4.11–10.66	7.04–9.57
9–10	1050–1335	9.67–12.01	62–72	8.32–12.12	9.02–13.93	8.41–10.81
11–CCR	1185–1385	11.20–14.10	67–74	10.34–14.2	12.30–14.50	9.57–12

Source: CCSSO, 2012.

Computers use mathematical formulae to estimate difficulty. Teachers and parents focus on ideas that will confuse the reader or be inappropriate for students at a given age. Furthermore, teachers use their knowledge of text structures to identify areas of difficulty which will require instruction.

Qualitative factors of texts include (Fisher et al., 2012; NGA & CCSSO, 2010b) the following.

- **Levels of meaning and purpose:** Such as the density and complexity of the information, use of figurative language, and stated and implied purposes

- **Structure:** Including the text's genre, organization, narration, and use of text features and graphics

- **Language conventionality and clarity:** Especially in its use of English language variations and registers

- **Knowledge demands:** Including the assumed background knowledge, prior knowledge, cultural knowledge, and vocabulary knowledge

Qualitative factors can make a text more or less complex, and they cannot be measured quantitatively. For instance, the book *Raising Sweetness* (Stanley, 1999) has a Lexile scale score of 530, situating it near the lower end of the grade 2–3 band. But the text's extensive use of the southwestern U.S. cowboy dialect makes this much more difficult for some readers to understand. In addition, the book requires extensive cultural knowledge about cowboys and the Old West. Assessment of text complexity using these factors is an excellent task for members of a collaborative team who are experienced with using a text and are familiar with a specific text's structure.

Using the rubric in table 2.2 (page 35), a fifth-grade team met to discuss informational texts for use in class. The team members turned their attention to *We Are the Ship: The Story of the Negro Baseball Leagues* (Nelson, 2008), an informational text with a Lexile score of 900L. The team identified several aspects of the book that would make it more or less difficult. It notes that the book was told from the perspective of a grandfather recounting his memories to his grandchildren, a factor that made the narration more understandable. In addition, text features, like illustrations, reinforce the powerful tone of the narration. However, the team members soon agreed that the levels of meaning ultimately made the book more complex. The team recognized that the density of information in each of the stories was evidenced in its sentence structure, especially the number of dependent clauses. In addition, the stories themselves spoke to a level of institutional racism that students might not immediately perceive. By identifying what made the text more complex, team members were able to design their instruction around reading dense text, identifying multiple levels of meaning, and establishing the author's purpose.

The third dimension for determining text complexity concerns the match between the reader and the task (NGA & CCSSO, 2010b). Factors that are internal to the reader include his or her cognitive capabilities, motivation, knowledge, and experiences. The task demand also influences the relative difficulty of the text. Teacher-led tasks, such as an interactive read-aloud, provide a high degree of scaffolding and make an otherwise difficult text much more comprehensible. Peer-led tasks, such as a small-group literature circle discussion, provide a moderate level of scaffolding as students collaborate to understand the task. Individual tasks, such as independent reading, provide the least amount of scaffolding and place most of the responsibility on the reader's shoulders. In order for students to progress toward increasingly more complex texts, they need a mixture of all of these tasks (Fisher et al., 2012). An over-reliance on one level of task difficulty occurs at the expense of others and can stymie a student's progress. This is perhaps the ongoing discussion collaborative planning teams should have as they design instruction with specific students in mind.

While the anchor standards for reading ground the grade-level standards, there is some overlap in grade levels as it pertains to text exemplars. You may recall that the exemplars are organized somewhat differently to reflect the developmental nature of reading. Therefore, the text exemplars are categories across grades 2–3, with a separate list for grades 4–5 (NGA & CCSSO, 2010c). Because of this, it is wise for third-grade teachers to devote some time to discussing text complexity with their second-grade colleagues. This will ensure agreement in regard to identifying those texts that are considered to be at the lower end of the grade band (second grade), with those at the higher level (third grade).

The anchor standards, and the grade-level standards that follow them, are far too complex to teach in a single lesson or to teach in isolation. Keeping this concept in mind is important as collaborative team members examine these standards for in-depth reading. It is the interaction of these standards within and across domains that makes them powerful. To divide and then reassemble them as isolated lessons will undermine the enduring understandings the standards articulate. The overarching goal should be to teach the habits of effective communicators, and to avoid isolated strategy instruction (Frey, Fisher, & Berkin, 2008).

Table 2.2: Qualitative Factors of Text Complexity

	3 Points (Stretch) Texts Stretch a Reader or Require Instruction	2 Points (Grade Level) Texts That Require Grade-Appropriate Skills	1 Point (Comfortable) Texts That Are Comfortable or Build Background, Fluency, and Skills
Levels of Meaning and Purpose			
Density and Complexity	Text has significant density and complexity, with multiple levels of meaning; meanings may be more ambiguous.	Text has a single, but more complex or abstract level of meaning; some meanings are stated, while others are left to the reader to identify.	Text has single and literal levels of meaning; meaning is explicitly stated.
Figurative Language	Figurative language plays a significant role in identifying the meaning of the text; more sophisticated figurative language is used (irony and satire, allusions, archaic or less familiar symbolism); the reader is left to interpret these meanings.	Figurative language such as imagery, metaphors, symbolism, and personification are used to make connections within the text to more explicit information, and readers are supported in understanding these language devices through examples and explanations.	There is a limited use of symbolism, metaphors, and poetic language that allude to other unstated concepts; language is explicit and relies on literal interpretations.
Purpose	The purpose is deliberately withheld from the reader, who must use other interpretive skills to identify it.	The purpose is implied but is easily identified based on title or context.	The purpose or main idea is directly and explicitly stated at the beginning of the reading.
Structure			
Genre	Genre is unfamiliar or bends and expands the rules for the genre.	Genre is either unfamiliar but is a reasonable example or it is a familiar genre that bends and expands the rules for the genre.	Genre is familiar and the text is consistent with the elements of that genre.

continued →

	3 Points (Stretch) Texts Stretch a Reader or Require Instruction	2 Points (Grade Level) Texts That Require Grade-Appropriate Skills	1 Point (Comfortable) Texts That Are Comfortable or Build Background, Fluency, and Skills
Structure			
Organization	The organization distorts time or sequence in a deliberate effort to delay the reader's full understanding of the plot, process, or set of concepts; may include significant flashbacks, foreshadowing, or shifting perspectives.	The organization adheres to most conventions, but digresses on occasion to temporarily shift the reader's focus to another point of view, event, time, or place, before returning to the main idea or topic.	The organization is conventional, sequential, or chronological, with clear signals and transitions to lead the reader through a story, process, or set of concepts.
Narration	An unreliable narrator provides a distorted or limited view to the reader; the reader must use other clues to deduce the truth; multiple narrators provide conflicting information; shifting points of view keep the reader guessing.	Third-person limited or first-person narration provides accurate, but limited perspectives or viewpoints.	Third-person omniscient narration or an authoritative and credible voice provides an appropriate level of detail and keeps little hidden from the view of the reader.
Text Features and Graphics	There is limited use of text features to organize information and guide the reader. Information in the graphics is not repeated in the main part of the text but is essential for understanding the text.	Has a wider array of text features including margin notes, diagrams, graphs, font changes, and other devices that compete for the reader's attention; graphics and visuals are used to augment and illustrate information in the main part of the text.	Text features (such as bold and italicized words, headings, and subheadings) organize information explicitly and guide the reader; graphics or illustrations may be present but are not necessary to understand the main part of the text.
Language Conventionality and Clarity			
Standard English and Variations	The text includes significant and multiple styles of English and its variations, and these are unfamiliar to the reader.	Some distance exists between the reader's linguistic base and the language conventions used in the text; the vernacular used is unfamiliar to the reader.	The language closely adheres to the reader's linguistic base.

Register	The register is archaic, formal, domain specific, or scholarly.	The register is consultative or formal, and may be academic but acknowledges the developmental level of the reader.	The register is casual and familiar.
Knowledge Demands			
Background Knowledge	The text places demands on the reader that extend far beyond his or her experiences, and provides little in the way of explanation of these divergent experiences.	There is distance between the reader's experiences and those in the text, but there is acknowledgement of these divergent experiences, and sufficient explanation to bridge the gaps.	The text contains content that closely matches the reader's life experiences.
Prior Knowledge	Presumes specialized or technical content knowledge and little in the way of review or explanation of these concepts is present in the text.	Requires subject-specific knowledge, but the text augments this with review or summary of this information.	The prior knowledge needed to understand the text is familiar, and it draws on a solid foundation of practical, general, and academic learning.
Cultural Knowledge	The text relies on extensive or unfamiliar intertextuality and uses artifacts and symbols that reference archaic or historical cultures.	The text primarily references contemporary and popular culture to anchor explanations for new knowledge; intertextuality is used more extensively but is mostly familiar to the reader.	The reader uses familiar cultural templates to understand the text with limited or familiar intertextuality.
Vocabulary Knowledge	Vocabulary demand is extensive, domain specific, and representative of complex ideas; the text offers little in the way of context clues to support the reader.	Vocabulary draws on domain specific, general academic, and multiple meaning words, with text supports to guide the reader's correct interpretations of meanings; the vocabulary represents familiar concepts and ideas.	Vocabulary is controlled and uses the most commonly held meanings; multiple meaning words are used in a limited fashion.

Source: Adapted from Fisher et al., 2012.

Visit go.solution-tree.com/commoncore for a reproducible version of this table.

In the following sections, we will examine the Reading strand's parts—Literature, Informational Text, and Foundational Skills—across grades 3–5. The grade band is an essential vantage point for viewing and discussing the CCSS, precisely because it prevents the silo effect that can occur when grade levels operate independently from one another. While grade-level planning must occur in the collaborative teams, the work of the professional learning community at the school level should first and foremost foster communication and collaboration across grades in order to maximize the potential that the anchor standards afford.

Reading Standards for Literature in Grades 3–5

This part is linked directly to narrative text types—poems, drama, and stories, including folktales, fantasy, and realistic fiction. Although nonfiction biographies and autobiographies often use a narrative structure, they are situated as a type of informational text. Students in elementary school are traditionally exposed to a high volume of literature, although genres like poetry, drama, and folktales are often reserved for specific genre studies units, and used more rarely across the school year. Table 2.3 contains sample titles from the text exemplars in appendix B of the Common Core State Standards (NGA & CCSSO, 2010c).

Table 2.3: Exemplars for Literature Texts in Grades 3–5

Genre	Grade 3	Grade 4	Grade 5
Stories	MacLachlan (1985): *Sarah, Plain and Tall*	Farley (2008): *The Black Stallion* (original 1941)	Curtis (1999): *Bud, Not Buddy*
Poetry	Lathem (1979): "Stopping by Woods on a Snowy Evening" in *The Poetry of Robert Frost: The Collected Poems* (original 1923)	Blake (1971): "The Ecchoing Green" in *Songs of Innocence* (original 1789)	Ferris (1957): "The New Colossus" in *Favorite Poems Old and New* (original 1883)
Read-Aloud Stories	White (2001): *Charlotte's Web* (original 1952)	n/a	n/a
Read-Aloud Poetry	Fleischman (1988): "Fireflies" in *Joyful Noise: Poems for Two Voices*	n/a	n/a

Source: Adapted from NGA & CCSSO, 2010c.

The standards for literature for each grade level are drawn directly from the anchor standards and are organized in the same manner: Key Ideas and Details, Craft and Structure, Integration of Knowledge and Ideas, and Range of Reading and Level of Text Complexity. We invite you and your collaborative team to discuss the standards using the four-part-protocol described in figure 2.1 (page 30): (1) What is familiar? (2) What is new? (3) What may be challenging for students? (4) What may be challenging for teachers? (Visit **go.solution-tree.com/commoncore** for an online-only reproducible you can use to conduct analyses of other standards with your collaborative team.) We will share observations of our own to seed your discussions.

Key Ideas and Details in Literature

Table 2.4 lists the grades 3–5 standards for this domain. The standards contain many expected elements, as well as some more challenging demands that have implications for instruction.

Table 2.4: Literature Standards for Domain Key Ideas and Details, Grades 3–5

Anchor Standards	Grade 3 Standards	Grade 4 Standards	Grade 5 Standards
R.CCR.1: Read closely to determine what the text says explicitly and to make logical inferences from it; cite specific textual evidence when writing or speaking to support conclusions drawn from the text.	**RL.3.1:** Ask and answer questions to demonstrate understanding of a text, referring explicitly to the text as the basis for the answers.	**RL.4.1:** Refer to details and examples in a text when explaining what the text says explicitly and when drawing inferences from the text.	**RL.5.1:** Quote accurately from a text when explaining what the text says explicitly and when drawing inferences from the text.
R.CCR.2: Determine central ideas or themes of a text and analyze their development; summarize the key supporting details and ideas.	**RL.3.2:** Recount stories, including fables, folktales, and myths from diverse cultures; determine the central message, lesson, or moral and explain how it is conveyed through key details in the text.	**RL.4.2:** Determine a theme of a story, drama, or poem from details in the text; summarize the text.	**RL.5.2:** Determine a theme of a story, drama, or poem from details in the text, including how characters in a story or drama respond to challenges or how the speaker in a poem reflects upon a topic; summarize the text.
R.CCR.3: Analyze how and why individuals, events, and ideas develop and interact over the course of a text.	**RL.3.3:** Describe characters in a story (such as their traits, motivations, or feelings) and explain how their actions contribute to the sequence of events.	**RL.4.3:** Describe in depth a character, setting, or event in a story or drama, drawing on specific details in the text (such as a character's thoughts, words, or actions).	**RL.5.3:** Compare and contrast two or more characters, settings, or events in a story or drama, drawing on specific details in the text (such as how characters interact).

Source: Adapted from NGA & CCSSO, 2010, pp. 10 and 12.

Anchor standard two (R.CCR.2) highlights the importance of being able to recount stories from specific genres in third grade, with an expectation that this will be further developed in fourth and fifth grades as identifying themes. This is linked to the expectations for anchor standard three (R.CCR.3) that students in third and fourth grades are able to describe how story elements, such as character and setting, relate to both the explicit and implicit aspects of the story. By fifth grade, students are weighing the similarities and differences between two elements in the story. These are for the most part aligned with current practice and in all likelihood feel familiar.

However, anchor standard one (R.CCR.1) represents a shift in practice, as it introduces how to regularly use textual evidence to support conclusions. In third grade, this is mostly accomplished by requiring students to find explicitly stated information; in fourth and fifth grades, this practice is further expanded to include inferences. Citing evidence from the text can be a challenge for students who have become accustomed to stating their thoughts and opinions without referring back to the text. Building the habit of referring to the text requires a shift in instruction, especially in our questioning habits. Regularly using text-based questions can drive young readers back to the text and reinforce selective re-reading and look-backs as methods to support deeper comprehension (Bossert & Schwantes, 1996).

Remembering to ask text-dependent questions requires preparation. After all, it is much easier to ask more general questions about a selection, especially the kind that allows students to make personal connections. However, these don't advance student knowledge of the reading itself and can derail classroom discussions about a text. As depicted in figure 2.2 (page 41), there are six types of questions that require students to use evidence from the text in their responses.

These questions represent a progression of increasingly more complex understandings, with literal-level knowledge forming the foundation as they move toward inferential meaning and critical analysis.

1. **General understanding questions:** Teachers pose these questions to determine whether students grasp the overall meaning of the text. While they may appear more global in nature, they are created so that students are required to *explain* as well as *describe*. Ms. Martinez asks a general understanding question of her third-grade students who were reading *If the World Were a Village* (Smith, 2002) when she asks, "Why does the author use a village of one hundred people to present this information?" Shaylene responds, "It's because the real numbers are so big!" Hector adds, "And it helps us see what most people do for work. And it show that most people are in Asia."

2. **Key detail questions:** These questions build on the foundational knowledge needed for general understanding by drawing attention to critical details that relate to the whole. Ms. Martinez asks, "How many real people does each person represent in our imaginary village?" Manny answers, "It says on page seven that each person in the village is the same as 62,000,000 in the real world."

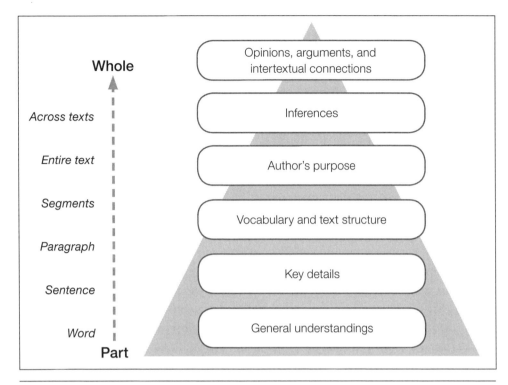

Figure 2.2: Progression of text-dependent questions.

3. **Vocabulary and text structure questions:** These questions bridge the literal level meanings of a text to move toward inferential interpretations. Questions regarding word choice, use of figurative language, and organization of information further build students' understanding of the author's craft. Ms. Martinez asks a question about the text's structure: "You can't read this book like a story, with a beginning, a middle, and an end. What are you noticing about the way this book is organized?" The class discusses the fact that each page represents a different category, such as nationality and age. In addition, the students notice the pattern of information—especially that each features numbers that add up to 100. At each turn, Ms. Martinez presses them to provide examples from the text.

4. **Author's purpose questions:** Invite students to step back from the text in order to examine the reading's effect on an audience and to look closely for clues that illuminate the author's intentions. These questions may focus on genre and narration, or require students to engage in critical analysis in determining whether another viewpoint is missing. The text type itself shapes the author's purpose questions. Ms. Martinez, knowing that this is an informational book with a persuasive message, wants her students to examine the author's purpose. "David Smith tells you directly why he's writing this book. Did you notice that?" Her students search the text again, and Mario says, "He wants us to find out about our neighbors." She probes, "Why does he want us

to know this? Keep digging." Renate finds it, and says, "He wants us to know about problems people have. He says that there are problems with people not having enough water." Mario adds, "And electricity." Renate finishes, "And some kids don't get to go to school."

5. **Inferencing questions:** These questions further the progression toward deeper understanding by requiring students to locate the nuances of a literary text, examine the arguments contained in a persuasive piece, or probe the details of major ideas in an informational text passage. One of the inference questions Ms. Martinez asks relates to the world's growing population. She draws students' attention to the information that for every one person in the village who dies, three are born. "So if our village always stays at one hundred people, what needs to change in our math?" she asks. This is a difficult concept for her students to understand and requires several minutes of discussion. But eventually students begin to see that the number each person in the imaginary village represents will have to increase. "So it gets bigger than 62,000,000 all the time!" Amal exclaims, "I wonder what it is now." Ms. Martinez is pleased that her class is wrestling with this complex idea. "'Cause that has to mean that the Earth is getting really crowded!" Mario marvels.

6. **Opinions, arguments, and intertextual connection questions:** These questions advance students' thinking about the broader meanings of a text by foregrounding it against a backdrop of personal experiences and inviting comparisons across texts. When these questions are delayed until after students have had a chance to read and re-read a text, the discussions themselves are richer and more complex. Ms. Martinez encourages her students to develop a question they still had after reading the passage on religions. Pedro's group states it wants to find out what religions U.S. residents practice and how they compare with the rest of the world.

Although these examples come from an informational text, comparable questions are just as useful with literary text. Fifth-grade teacher Arletta Strong uses text-dependent questions with her students, many of whom are English learners.

"Our team chose *Because of Winn-Dixie* (DiCamillo, 2000) for several reasons. The grade-level readability is fourth grade, which seemed like a good place to start the school year. We have lots of English learners, so I wanted to back down the readability just a bit so we could pay closer attention to the qualitative factors in this book," she says. "There's lots of inferring they need to do to understand the story." She joins a literature circle group of six students after it read and discussed the first chapter.

"I've got some questions of my own, and I want you to use your book as you think about them," she says. "Don't ever think that being an effective reader means you have to keep everything in your head. I want you to look back. So let's start with the title. Why did India, the main character, name the dog Winn-Dixie?"

Souvann responds, "She was at the store when she met the dog for the first time." "Yes, that's true," Ms. Strong replies. "But can you find the place in the book where she explains it? Look on page ten." Souvann searches the text and finds it. "Here it is. I didn't know what his name was, so I just said the first thing that came into my head." "There you go!" Ms. Strong exclaims. "And your first answer is a great example of inferring. The author didn't say this outright, but you were drawing conclusions on your own. So now another question. How does India know the dog is friendly? Remember to use your book."

This time, Taahira responds, "It says on page eight, 'He was having a good time.' And in the next sentence, 'He was wagging his tail.'" Paolo interjects, "'And he smiled right at me.' That's in the next sentence." "And look on the next page," Ms. Strong suggests. "Can you find more evidence?" Souvann responds, "When the store manager fell, 'The dog leaned over him, real concerned, and licked his face.'"

After briefly discussing the outward behaviors of a friendly dog, Ms. Strong returns to her questions. "India makes a big decision, one that is going to set up the entire story. What decision does she make, and why is it a risky one?"

For the next few minutes, the group discusses the character's decision to pretend the dog belongs to her and anticipates that she is probably going to have to talk one or both of her parents into keeping the dog. They maintain that this is going to be difficult, especially since the dog is dirty. "And at my house, all dogs are dirty! We would never let one in!" says Taahira. Ms. Strong asks the girl to explain further, and Taahira explains that in her culture dogs are outside working animals, not pets. At the conclusion of their literature circle discussion, she asks the students to write a brief summary in their journal about the first chapter and make some predictions about what might happen next.

"I'm still getting to know them as learners," Ms. Strong tells her collaborative team members, "And these journal entries give me a sense of their comprehension." She explains how when she reviewed their writing, students were accurately predicting that India was going to have to convince her parents about why she should be allowed to keep the dog. "I think Taahira's comments pushed their thinking. They're all convinced that India is going to have to give some good, practical reasons if she's going to convince anyone," she says.

Craft and Structure in Literature

The language of structure in literature dominates this domain (see table 2.5, page 44). In this grade band, students are acquiring domain-specific tier three (Beck et al., 2002) vocabulary terms such as *stanza*, *scene*, and *stage direction*, as well as identifying the use of similes, metaphors, and other figurative language. Fourth grade can be especially challenging, as students connect words and phrases with mythological roots, like *colossal*, *jovial*, and *narcissistic*. In addition, the fourth-grade standards also require students to understand the language of poetic structures, which may be something that

Table 2.5: Literature Standards for Domain Craft and Structure, Grades 3–5

Anchor Standards	Grade 3 Standards	Grade 4 Standards	Grade 5 Standards
R.CCR.4: Interpret words and phrases as they are used in a text, including determining technical, connotative, and figurative meanings, and analyze how specific word choices shape meaning or tone.	**RL.3.4:** Determine the meaning of words and phrases as they are used in a text, distinguishing literal from nonliteral language.	**RL.4.4:** Determine the meaning of words and phrases as they are used in a text, including those that allude to significant characters found in mythology (such as Herculean).	**RL.5.4:** Determine the meaning of words and phrases as they are used in a text, including figurative language like metaphors and similes.
R.CCR.5: Analyze the structure of texts, including how specific sentence, paragraphs, and larger portions of the text (like a section, chapter, scene, or stanza) relate to each other and the whole.	**RL.3.5:** Refer to parts of stories, dramas, and poems when writing or speaking about a text, using terms such as chapter, scene, and stanza; describe how each successive part builds on earlier sections.	**RL.4.5:** Explain major differences between poems, drama, and prose, and refer to the structural elements of poems (like verse, rhythm, and meter) and drama (like casts of characters, settings, descriptions, dialogue, and stage directions) when writing or speaking about a text.	**RL.5.5:** Explain how a series of chapters, scenes, or stanzas fits together to provide the overall structure of a particular story, drama, or poem.
R.CCR.6: Assess how point of view or purpose shapes the content and style of a text.	**RL.3.6:** Distinguish their own point of view from that of the narrator or those of the characters.	**RL.4.6:** Compare and contrast the point of view from which different stories are narrated, including the difference between first- and third-person narrations.	**RL.5.6:** Describe how a narrator's or speaker's point of view influences how events are described.

Source: Adapted from NGA & CCSSO, 2010a, pp. 10 and 12.

has not been routinely taught in the past. Across the grade band, students deepen their understanding of point of view, first from their own standpoint, as well as the characters they encounter.

Fourth-grade teacher Jim Otterbein uses Emma Lazarus's poem "The New Colossus" (Ferris, 1957) to ensure that his students are familiar with the most widely known use of this poem—on the Statue of Liberty. They read *Lady Liberty: A Biography* (Rappaport, 2008), an informational book written in poetic form.

"This gave them some excellent background information about the Statue of Liberty and its construction, as well as why Lazarus's poem was carved onto the tablet Lady Liberty holds," Mr. Otterbein says in a collaborative team discussion. Using these two texts, he teaches about poetic form, the content of the message in the poem, and its symbolism for the United States. In addition, students need to understand Greek mythology in order to fully appreciate the title and the first lines of "The New Colossus":

> Not like the brazen giant of Greek fame,
>
> With conquering limbs astride from land to land.

Mr. Otterbein explains, "We looked at illustrations of the Colossus of Rhodes and why it was built as a symbol to frighten people away. We discussed why Lazarus called this 'The New Colossus' as a way of contrasting this with the welcoming message of the Statue of Liberty."

Mr. Otterbein plans to return to this poem later in the school year. "We'll be studying the importance of immigrants to the development of our state and region," he says. "And we'll examine this poem again to discuss the ways our nation lives up to these ideals at times, and when it hasn't."

Integration of Knowledge and Ideas in Literature

Only two of the three anchor standards in this domain appear in the Literature part, as argumentation is not commonly utilized in fiction (see table 2.6, page 46). There are familiar elements in this domain, especially the emphasis in anchor standard nine (R.CCR.9) on author study in third grade. In contrast, fourth grade's emphasis on mythology continues with thematic analyses of archetypes in literature, such as good and evil, and the quest as a storytelling device. A more familiar application of this is the Cinderella story archetype that appears in the oral and written traditions of so many cultures. A likely challenge will be to incorporate other archetypes for students. For example, a study of the role of the quest as a storytelling device might include *The Wonderful Wizard of Oz* (Baum, 2000), which is a literature read-aloud text exemplar for third grade, *The Giver* (Lowry, 1993), and *The Incredible Journey* (Burnford, 1997). These and stories like them provide students with understanding who the questers are, the obstacles they face, and the abettors who help them.

The focus on visual literacy in anchor standard seven (R.CCR.7) is likely to represent a genuine departure from what most elementary educators teach. While extraction of information from illustrations is common in the primary grades, the dominance of text in the middle and upper grades often means that this form of literacy is neglected. In fifth grade, multiliteracies take a front seat. Movement, light, sound, and images comprise these elements (Frey, Fisher, & Gonzalez, 2010).

Fifth-grade teacher Melinda Townsend has developed a comparative study of the graphic novel *The Invention of Hugo Cabret* (Selznick, 2007) and its film adaptation, *Hugo* (King, Headington, Scorsese, Depp, & Scorsese, 2011), with her students.

Table 2.6: Literature Standards for Domain Integration of Knowledge and Ideas, Grades 3–5

Anchor Standards	Grade 3 Standards	Grade 4 Standards	Grade 5 Standards
R.CCR.7: Integrate and evaluate content presented in diverse media and formats, including visually and quantitatively, as well as words.	**RL.3.7:** Explain how specific aspects of a text's illustrations contribute to what is conveyed by the words in a story (such as how they create mood or emphasize aspects of a character or setting).	**RL.4.7:** Make connections between the text of a story or drama and a visual or oral presentation of the text, identifying where each version reflects specific descriptions and directions in the text.	**RL.5.7:** Analyze how visual and multimedia elements contribute to the meaning, tone, or beauty of a text (such as a graphic novel, multimedia presentation of fiction, folktale, myth, or poem).
R.CCR.8: Delineate and evaluate the argument and specific claims in a text, including the validity of the reasoning as well as the relevance and sufficiency of the evidence.	n/a	n/a	n/a
R.CCR.9: Analyze how two or more texts address similar themes or topics in order to build knowledge or to compare the approaches the authors take.	**RL.3.9:** Compare and contrast the themes, settings, and plots of stories written by the same author about the same or similar characters (such as in books from a series).	**RL.4.9:** Compare and contrast the treatment of similar themes and topics (such as the opposition of good and evil) and patterns of events (like a quest) in stories, myths, and traditional literature from different cultures.	**RL.5.9:** Compare and contrast stories in the same genre (such as mysteries and adventure stories) on their approaches to similar themes and topics.

Source: Adapted from NGA & CCSSO, 2010a, pp. 10 and 12.

"After reading the book, we analyzed segments of the film, comparing the illustrations in the book with shots in the film," she says. "The book can be seen as a storyboard for the film, and the film in turn takes Selnick's static images and reinterprets them through movement. By comparing the two, they can more fully appreciate how images, whether they are still or moving, can tell a story."

Range of Reading and Level of Text Complexity in Literature

Anchor standard ten (R.CCR.10) in this domain is brief but heavily influences much of the instruction across all the domains and other standards. Looking at the grades 3–5 band, one can see how text complexity and scaffolded instruction intersect (see table 2.7). The third-grade standard references the grades 2–3 text exemplars and further notes that students should be able to read similar stories and poems "at the high end of the . . . band independently and proficiently" (NGA & CCSSO, 2010a, p. 12). The grades 2–3 band is further defined as 420–820L (Lexile range). This range is broader than that MetaMetrics's previously defined for the 2–3 grade-level band (450–720L). Similarly, the grades 4–5 band has been raised from 645–845L to a new range of 740–1010L. As noted in table 2.1 (page 33), these are revised measures for Common Core ELA (CCSSO, 2012).

These text complexity levels are likely to be challenging for many students, but keep in mind that these are end-of-year expectations. As well, merely giving students difficult texts and then expecting them to somehow read them is a sure recipe for failure (Allington, 2002). In order for students to be able to read and comprehend more difficult texts, they require purposeful instruction that relies on a gradual release of responsibility model of instruction (Frey, Fisher, & Nelson, 2010; Pearson & Gallagher, 1983).

Table 2.7: Literature Standards for Domain Range of Reading and Text Complexity, Grades 3–5

Anchor Standard	Grade 3 Standard	Grade 4 Standard	Grade 5 Standard
	Lexile Range: 420–820L* (grade 2–3 band)	Lexile Range: 740–1010L* (grade 4–5 band)	
R.CCR.10: Read and comprehend complex literary and informational texts independently and proficiently.	RL.3.10: By the end of the year, read and comprehend literature, including stories, dramas, and poetry, at the high end of the grades 2–3 text complexity band independently and proficiently.	RL.4.10: By the end of the year, read and comprehend literature, including stories, dramas, and poetry in the grades 4–5 text complexity band proficiently, with scaffolding as needed at the high end of the range.	RL.5.10: By the end of the year, read and comprehend literature, including stories, dramas, and poetry at the high end of the grades 4–5 text complexity band independently and proficiently.

* This is a quantitative measure only. Full assessment of text complexity must also include qualitative factors and reader and task considerations.

Source: Adapted from NGA & CCSSO, 2010a, pp. 10 and 12.

Reading Standards for Informational Text in Grades 3–5

The Reading Standards for Informational Text parallel the Reading Standards for Literature. These standards describe the uses of content-rich nonfiction trade books that focus on a concept or topic, biographies and autobiographies, photographic essays, procedural texts, and texts that draw from primary-source documents (Moss, 2003). Informational texts can and should be used across disciplines, not only in the reading and language arts block, as they are equally as valuable for building content knowledge as they are as materials for reading instruction. Like the literature exemplars in appendix B of the CCSS (NGA & CCSSO, 2010c), informational text exemplars are organized as a grades 2–3 band, and a separate grades 4–5 band. The difference between the two lists centers on the inclusion of read-aloud examples for the lower grades. The text exemplars do not include read-aloud examples above grade 3. This does not mean that teachers should abandon read-alouds as an instructional approach but rather that students in the primary grades need time to develop their independent reading habits and skills. Table 2.8 lists example texts.

Table 2.8: Exemplars for Informational Texts in Grades 3–5

Genre	Grade 3	Grade 4	Grade 5
Informational Texts	Aliki (1986): *A Medieval Feast*	Montgomery (2006): *Quest for the Tree Kangaroo: An Expedition to the Cloud Forest of New Guinea*	Otfinoski (1996): *The Kid's Guide to Money: Earning It, Saving It, Spending It, Growing It, Sharing It*
Read-Aloud Informational Texts	D'Aluisio and Menzel (2008): *What the World Eats*	n/a	n/a

Source: Adapted from NGA & CCSSO, 2010c.

As with the standards for literature, the informational text standards emanate from the same set of anchor standards. One noticeable difference is that anchor standard eight (R.CCR.8), which concerns argumentation, is represented in the Informational Text part. In the same fashion that your collaborative team analyzed the standards for reading and literature, we invite you to do so in this section using the four-part protocol described in figure 2.1 (page 30): (1) What is familiar? (2) What is new? (3) What may be challenging for students? (4) What may be challenging for teachers? (Visit **go.solution -tree.com/commoncore** for an online-only reproducible of figure 2.1 that you can use to for this analysis with your collaborative team.)

Key Ideas and Details in Informational Texts

The grade-level standards for this domain are similar to those for literature in the sense that they require students to locate explicitly stated information (grade 3), progressing to inferential meaning in grade 4, and being able to quote the text by grade 5 (see table 2.9). As a reminder, the use of text-based questions is especially valuable in encouraging students to engage in multiple readings. Re-reading is particularly important when students are reading conceptually dense informational texts. In addition, understanding the relationships between ideas, concepts, or events also grows across the three grades, with students examining the internal construction of the content knowledge as the author explains and discusses it.

Table 2.9: Informational Text Standards for Domain Key Ideas and Details, Grades 3–5

Anchor Standards	Grade 3 Standards	Grade 4 Standards	Grade 5 Standards
R.CCR.1: Read closely to determine what the text says explicitly and to make logical inferences from it; cite specific textual evidence when writing or speaking to support conclusions drawn from the text.	**RI.3.1:** Ask and answer questions to demonstrate understanding of a text, referring explicitly to the text as the basis for answers.	**RI.4.1:** Refer to details and examples in a text when explaining what the text says explicitly and when drawing inferences from the text.	**RI.5.1:** Quote accurately from a text when explaining what the text says explicitly and when drawing inferences from the text.
R.CCR.2: Determine central ideas or themes of a text and analyze their development; summarize the key supporting details and ideas.	**RI.3.2:** Determine the main idea of a text; recount the key details and explain how they support the main idea.	**RI.4.2:** Determine the main idea of a text and explain how it is supported by key details; summarize the text.	**RI.5.2:** Determine two or more main ideas of a text and explain how they are supported by key details; summarize the text.
R.CCR.3: Analyze how and why individuals, events, and ideas develop and interact over the course of the text.	**RI.3.3:** Describe the relationship between a series of historical events, scientific ideas or concepts, or steps in technical procedures in a text, using language that pertains to time, sequence, and cause and effect.	**RI.4.3:** Explain events, procedures, ideas, or concepts in a historical, scientific, or technical text, including what happened and why, based on specific information in the text.	**RI.5.3:** Explain the relationships or interactions between two or more individuals, events, ideas, or concepts in a historical, scientific, or technical text based on specific information in the text.

Source: Adapted from NGA & CCSSO, 2010a, pp. 10 and 14.

Fourth-grade science teacher Julia Washington uses short articles from the weekly science magazine her school subscribes to with her students. News about a discovery regarding bee colony collapse disorder caused quite a bit of conversation.

"We've been interested in bees all year," she says. "It started with our unit on pollination and seed dispersal, and took off from there." The class had been following reports of the mysterious disappearance of honeybees in their county and state. "We're in a major agricultural area, and this affects the livelihood of so many of their families," Ms. Washington notes.

Throughout the year, the class consults the county's website to follow local developments. When the class's weekly science newspaper arrives with news about a report that perhaps pesticides may be harming the bees, the students were interested to learn more. Ms. Washington says, "We read the article first to get an overall sense of its meaning, and then went back to examine the way the information was presented. There were lots of qualifications in there, and so we looked for statements that contained words and phrases like *perhaps, it is possible,* and *maybe*. It helped us focus on what science is often about—exploring possible answers and understanding what conclusions we can, and cannot, draw. I want them to be good consumers of scientific information, and paying close attention to these details makes them better able to understand the details and prevent them from making sweeping generalizations that are incorrect."

Craft and Structure in Informational Texts

This domain emphasizes the importance of general and domain-specific words and phrases within a larger piece of text, and the organizational structures and features that tie these to conceptual knowledge (see table 2.10). Anchor standard five (R.CCR.5) deserves special attention, as it highlights text features in grade 3 and introduces fourth-grade readers to text structures such as chronological order, problem and solution, cause and effect, and compare and contrast. By grade 5, students are utilizing the text structure itself to understand multiple points of view or accounts of a historical event.

Fifth-grade teacher Jennie Abramowitz uses *Dateline: Troy* (Fleischman, 1996) with her students to explore multiple points of view in a historical text.

"The fifth-grade teachers chose this book based on all the elements of text complexity," she offers to her vertical collaborative team members. "With an 860 Lexile score, we had a good first measure of its appropriateness for our students. We also looked at the way the text is structured—you know, the qualitative stuff." She went on to list the merits of this book, including its use of maps, newspaper clippings, and the bibliography at the end.

Previously, her collaborative planning team determined that the book was highly complex because of factors such as the use of archaic language conventions and complicated syntax. Ms. Abramowitz cites this sentence as an example of both: "Had Prince Palamedes not taken a sheep's knuckle bone and made the first pair of dice, the endless campaign might have driven them mad" (Fleischman, 1996, p. 40). "That's tough stuff,"

Table 2.10: Informational Text Standards for Domain Craft and Structure, Grades 3–5

Anchor Standards	Grade 3 Standards	Grade 4 Standards	Grade 5 Standards
R.CCR.4: Interpret words and phrases as they are used in a text, including determining technical, connotative, and figurative meanings, and analyze how specific word choices shape meaning and tone.	**RI.3.4:** Determine the meaning of general academic and domain-specific words and phrases in a text relevant to a grade 3 topic or subject area.	**RI.4.4:** Determine the meaning of general academic and domain-specific words or phrases in a text relevant to a grade 4 topic or subject area.	**RI.5.4:** Determine the meaning of general academic and domain-specific words and phrases in a text relevant to a grade 5 topic or subject area.
R.CCR.5: Analyze the structure of texts, including how specific sentences, paragraphs, and larger portions of the text (like a section, chapter, scene, or stanza) relate to each other and the style of a text.	**RI.3.5:** Use text features and search tools (like key words, sidebars, and hyperlinks) to locate information relevant to a given topic efficiently.	**RI.4.5:** Describe the overall structure (such as chronology, comparison, cause and effect, or problem and solution) of events, ideas, concepts, or information in a text or part of a text.	**RI.5.5:** Compare and contrast the overall structure (such as chronology, comparison, cause and effect, problem and solution) of events, ideas, concepts, or information in two or more texts.
R.CCR.6: Assess how point of view or purpose shapes the content and style of a text.	**RI.3.6:** Distinguish their own point of view from that of the author of a text.	**RI.4.6:** Compare and contrast a firsthand and secondhand account of the same event or topic; describe the differences in focus and the information provided.	**RI.5.6:** Analyze multiple accounts of the same event or topic, noting important similarities and differences in the point of view they represent.

Source: Adapted from NGA & CCSSO, 2010a, pp. 10 and 14.

she says. "The passive voice and the dependent clause make it harder to comprehend, and then you add things like 'driven mad' and 'sheep's knuckles'! It's going to take time to unpack sentences like this."

The team also made some decisions based on what teachers knew about their students and the tasks they would use to teach this information. "The fourth-grade team did a lot with them on mythology last year," she says. "Our social studies content is on U.S. history, and we want to be able to show them how accounts of ancient conflict parallel our own country's wars." The book recounts the Trojan War on the left page through text and juxtaposes images and newspaper accounts of similar developments in modern culture and of 20th century U.S. wars.

Ms. Abramowitz discusses two pages of text with her students using a close-reading approach (Fisher et al., 2012; Richards, 1929). A guided close reading of a worthy passage consists of:

- An initial independent reading to gain familiarity with the text

- Annotations of the text to note patterns, confusions, and connections

- Think-alouds to scaffold comprehension

- Text-based questions

- Discussion using evidence from the text

- Opportunities to re-read the passage, both in its entirety and using selective portions of the passage

In one lesson, the class focuses on a page recounting the Oath of Tyndareus, which states Helen of Troy's suitors will defend her chosen husband from any man who tries to steal her. Menelaus, Helen's husband, calls on the suitors at the start of the Trojan War. The opposite page has a newspaper clipping of a call to active duty for a group of U.S. Army reservists, who will be sent to Korea to counter the August 1950 North Korean invasion of Pohang. After briefly introducing the reading, the teacher moves students into small groups to *read with a pencil*, as Ms. Abramowitz calls it, underlining unfamiliar words and phrases and marking the text with arrows to signal connections. After students discuss the first reading with one another and then as a class, Ms. Abramowitz gains a sense of what she would need to model aloud for students.

She projects a copy of the text on a document camera and reads aloud while they follow silently. In the second paragraph, she comes to this passage: "To keep their swords sheathed, he'd proposed an oath: each suitor would swear to defend Helen's husband against any man who tried to steal her away. Since all had hoped to gain this protection, each of them had taken the oath" (Fleischman, 1996, p. 24). Ms. Abramowitz begins to think aloud. "I wasn't sure what *oath* meant, so I kept reading the next sentences," she says. "I'm seeing that it's about making a promise [circles *oath* and underlines *swear to defend*]. What I'm noticing is that the author is giving me more explanation of what the oath is, so that I can infer that it's a promise."

Later in the passage, she encounters the word *pledge* and links it to her previous statement. "Yep, that's another word for promise, and I'm feeling even surer that I know what an oath is," while simultaneously circling the words and drawing arrows between them.

A few minutes later, she asks text-based questions to foster discussion. "So when Helen disappears, the king gets really mad," she says. "So what's his response?" Aaron answers, "He calls all the guys to go fight to get Helen back." Ms. Abramowitz responds, "What makes you say that? Can you tell us where that is in the text?" Aaron replies, "It says, 'He sent heralds to all the former suitors, calling them to make good on their oaths.' I think a *herald* is like a messenger or something."

"So that gets us started, but I'm curious about the fighting part," Ms. Abramowitz notes. "How do you know?" "It's the next sentence," Aaron answers. "'Each would contribute soldiers or ships, making up a vast army and fleet.'" "There you go!" Ms. Abramowitz exclaims. "Does everyone see that?"

Integration of Knowledge and Ideas in Informational Texts

This domain highlights the importance of being able to extract and synthesize information from a variety of internal and external sources (see table 2.11, page 54). This includes being able to recognize signal words that contribute to the cohesion of a text. We often use the analogy of the poles used to mark a downhill skier's path as a way to illustrate the important contribution of signal words and transitional phrases to the cohesion of a text. Like these poles guide the skier, signal words and phrases illuminate a reader's path. Readers also extract information through illustrations, diagrams, and the like. Readers and skiers alike must continually monitor their surroundings for new information, as it informs the changing conditions. While the skier pays attention to the changes in the snow and ice on the trail and adjusts his or her performance accordingly, a reader must incorporate multiple sources of information to adjust his or her conceptual understanding.

Rana Takahashi, a third-grade science teacher, uses *Planet Earth/Inside Out* (Gibbons, 1995) with her students. At 800L, the book aligns quantitatively within the suggested grade band. In addition, the team's qualitative assessment notes that signal words were plentiful, and that the text was sectioned to correspond with the scientific illustrations.

"We looked for signal words and phrases, as well as ways the author compares and contrasts information," she says. "I'll give you an example." Turning to a page on the poles and equator, she points out contrastive information in the text: "'Also, it looks perfectly round—but it isn't. Instead it is slightly flat at its North and South Poles and bulges a little in its middle, which is called the *equator*'" (Gibbons, 1995, n.p.).

She continues, "After we talk about how Gail Gibbons uses a dash to set off the contrast, we look at the illustration. We can't see this flattening phenomenon, even though it tells us this in the text. Then we go back to the first part of the sentence, where it says, 'It looks perfectly round.' She's telling us you can't always believe your eyes alone. You have to look at other evidence as well."

Range of Reading and Level of Text Complexity in Informational Texts

With the exception of naming genres, the wording of standard ten in this domain is the same for informational texts as it is for literature (see table 2.12, page 55). As illustrated in previous examples, determining a text's complexity and then using it with other texts in such a way—using the staircase approach—so ideas build on one another is more complex.

Table 2.11: Informational Text Standards for Domain Integration of Knowledge and Ideas, Grades 3–5

Anchor Standards	Grade 3 Standards	Grade 4 Standards	Grade 5 Standards
R.CCR.7: Integrate and evaluate content presented in diverse media and formats, including visually and quantitatively, as well as in word.	**RI.3.7:** Use information gained from illustrations (like maps and photographs) and the words in a text to demonstrate understanding of the text (such as where, when, why, and how key events occur).	**RI.4.7:** Interpret information presented visually, orally, or quantitatively (such as in charts, graphs, diagrams, time lines, animations, or interactive elements on web pages) and explain how the information contributes to an understanding of the text in which it appears.	**RI.5.7:** Draw on information from multiple print or digital sources, demonstrating the ability to locate an answer to a question quickly or to solve a problem efficiently.
R.CCR.8: Delineate and evaluate the argument and specific claims in a text, including the validity of the reasoning as well as the relevance and sufficiency of the evidence.	**RI.3.8:** Describe the logical connection between particular sentences and paragraphs in a text (such as through comparison, cause and effect, or chronology).	**RI.4.8:** Explain how an author uses reasons and evidence to support particular points in a text.	**RI.5.8:** Explain how an author uses reasons and evidence to support particular points in a text, identifying which reasons and evidence support which points.
R.CCR.9: Analyze how two or more texts address similar themes or topics in order to build knowledge or to compare the approaches the authors take.	**RI.3.9:** Compare and contrast the most important points and key details presented in two texts on the same topic.	**RI.4.9:** Integrate information from two texts on the same topic in order to write or speak about the subject knowledgeably.	**RI.5.9:** Integrate information from several texts on the same topic in order to write or speak about the subject knowledgeably.

Source: Adapted from NGA & CCSSO, 2010a, pp. 10 and 14.

Teams must consider quantitative measures, qualitative factors, reader understanding, and task demand for informational texts.

Your collaborative team can begin to establish a sequence of texts across grades 3–5 by beginning with the texts already in use. Figure 2.3 (pages 56–57) is a protocol for teams to use as you make these determinations about text complexity. A good starting place to begin the conversation about text complexity is to refer to the text exemplars in appendix B of the Common Core State Standards (NGA & CCSSO, 2010c). Ideally, some of the texts already in use will appear on this list and can serve as placeholders for

Table 2.12: Informational Text Standards for Domain Range of Reading and Text Complexity, Grades 3–5

Anchor Standard	Grade 3 Standard	Grade 4 Standard	Grade 5 Standard
R.CCR.10: Read and comprehend complex literary and informational texts independently and proficiently.	**RI.3.10:** By the end of the year, read and comprehend informational texts, including history and social studies, science, and technical texts, at the high end of the grades 2–3 text complexity band independently and proficiently.	**RI.4.10:** By the end of the year, read and comprehend informational texts, including history and social studies, science, and technical texts, at the grades 4–5 text complexity band proficiently, with scaffolding as needed at the high end of the range.	**RI.4.10:** By the end of the year, read and comprehend informational texts, including history and social studies, science, and technical texts, at the high end of the grades 4–5 text complexity band independently and proficiently.

Source: Adapted from NGA & CCSSO, 2010a, pp. 10 and 14.

the texts team members have identified for further analysis. We suggest that the team discuss two or three texts at each meeting as a way to attune members to these considerations. As your team collectively becomes more adept at analyzing texts, pairs of teachers can collaborate to assess books for their text complexity and suggest recommendations for using them in class. Over time, the collaborative team can use these assessments to create a sequence of texts to be used at the beginning, middle, and end of each grade level in order to assure that texts are being used as a staircase from one year to the next.

Foundational Skills in Reading in Grades 3–5

The CCSS for reading in grades K–5 include a part, Foundational Skills, not featured in grades 6–12. As described in the Common Core ELA, these are not outcome standards, but rather necessary prerequisite skills for emergent, early, and intermediate readers. Therefore, they are not tied to the anchor standards like the grade-level expectations for Literature and Informational Text. Instead, these foundational skills are organized around what Scott G. Paris (2005) calls *constrained skills*. Certain early reading skills are fundamental to breaking the code of written language (Gentry, 2006). Readers must know the sounds of the language, alphabet of the language, the ways in which sounds are bolted onto the letters (National Institute of Child Health and Human Development, 2000). In reading terminology, we call these concepts *phonemic awareness*, *alphabetic knowledge*, and *phonological knowledge*. Some of these skills are finite, and therefore limited (or highly constrained): there are forty-four phonemes in the English language, and twenty-six letters in the alphabet. Sound and letter correspondence is broader but still somewhat limited. Fluency is also constrained, since at some point rate, pitch, intonation, and prosody converge to an end point at which reading can't go any faster. After all, you can and should only read so fast! On the other hand,

Title of text: _____

Author: _____ **Publication date:** _____

Current Experiences

What is the current use of the text? (Include grade level, content area, and unit or topic.)

What have our experiences been with using this text?

What are its positive outcomes?

What are its drawbacks?

Quantitative Measures

What is the quantitative measure of this text? What measure did we use?

Qualitative Factors

1 = Comfortable (texts that are comfortable or build background, fluency, and skills)

2 = Grade level (texts that require grade-appropriate skills)

3 = Stretch (texts that stretch a reader's thinking or require instruction)

Levels of Meaning and Purpose	Rating
Density and complexity	
Figurative language	
Purpose	
Score	

Structure	Rating
Genre	
Organization	
Narration	
Text features and graphics	
Score	

Language and Conventionality	Rating
Standard English and variations	
Register	
Score	

Knowledge Demands	Rating
Background knowledge	
Prior knowledge	
Cultural knowledge	
Vocabulary knowledge	
Score	
Total qualitative	

Questions for Considering the Reader and the Task

Will this text maintain our students' attention?

Will this text require specialized supports (such as language support or accommodations)?

Does the text's topic or genre interest our students?

Does the reader possess the needed metacognitive skills to comprehend the text?

Does the reader have sufficient background or prior knowledge to link to new information?

What direct experiences do our students have that may make this text more accessible?

Does this text require modeling of comprehension and word-solving strategies?

Does the task match the readers' collaborative learning and social skills?

Does the task provide sufficient challenge for our students, while avoiding protracted frustration?

Recommendations for Using This Text

For which grade is this text most appropriate, given the qualitative and quantitative analyses?

What are the specific teaching points necessary for student understanding?

Would this text be best for whole-class instruction, small-group learning, collaborative activities, or independent tasks?

Figure 2.3: Collaborative team protocol for determining text complexity.

Visit **go.solution-tree.com/commoncore** for a reproducible version of this figure.

unconstrained skills have no end point, and learning continues throughout a reader's lifetime. Vocabulary knowledge and comprehension are unconstrained. Think about it. Don't you know more vocabulary today than you did five years ago? Can't you comprehend text more ably now than when you were in college?

The K–5 Foundational Skills acknowledge the importance, as well as the end point, for constrained skills such as phonemic awareness and print concepts (like alphabetic knowledge, directionality, and spaces between words). These are features exclusively in the grades K–2 standards. Across grades K–5 are two other less-constrained skills: (1) phonics and word recognition and (2) fluency. These fully comprise the foundational skills in reading for grades 3–5.

Phonics and Word Recognition

In each grade level, there is a single, multifaceted standard (see table 2.13). Although brief, this core standard has implications for writing, spelling, and learning vocabulary. The emphasis in grade 3 is still on decoding—a sequence first established in the kindergarten standards. By fourth and fifth grade, it has morphed into word analysis, especially in using derivational knowledge of word origins and morphological knowledge to solve unfamiliar words. Throughout this grade band, the Common Core standards call attention to the importance of teaching the meanings of affixes (prefixes and suffixes), roots, and bases as part of word meaning. These are foundational for fostering the kind of structural analysis skills needed to solve unknown words and phrases. We will discuss these in more detail in the section on language in chapter 3.

Table 2.13: Reading Standards for Foundational Skills in Phonics and Word Recognition, Grades 3–5

Grade 3 Standards	Grade 4 Standards	Grade 5 Standards
RF.3.3: Know and apply grade-level phonics and word-analysis skills in decoding words.	**RF.4.3:** Know and apply grade-level phonics and word-analysis skills in decoding words.	**RF.5.3:** Know and apply grade-level phonics and word-analysis skills in decoding words.
a. Identify and know the meaning of the most common prefixes and derivational suffixes. b. Decode words with common Latin suffixes. c. Decode multisyllable words. d. Read grade-appropriate irregularly spelled words.	a. Use combined knowledge of all letter-sound correspondences, syllabication patterns, and morphology (like roots and affixes) to read accurately unfamiliar multisyllabic words in context and out of context.	a. Use combined knowledge of all letter-sound correspondences, syllabication patterns, and morphology (like roots and affixes) to read accurately unfamiliar multisyllabic words in context and out of context.

Source: Adapted from NGA & CCSSO, 2010a, p. 17.

Fluency

The ability to activate word-solving skills is necessary for fluency as well. Fluency (see table 2.14) is further described in terms of accuracy, rate, and prosody (the ability to read expressively). Taken together, these serve as a useful proxy for determining a young reader's comprehension (Rasinski, 2011). Fluency is assessed through oral- and silent-reading rates, but prosody can only be assessed though oral reading. An effective method for strengthening and assessing fluency and prosody is through *readers' theater*, an instructional approach in which students perform from a script that they have practiced collaboratively (Kinniburgh & Shaw, 2007).

Table 2.14: Reading Standards for Foundational Skills in Fluency, Grades 3–5

Grade 3 Standards	Grade 4 Standards	Grade 5 Standards
RF.3.4: Read with sufficient accuracy and fluency to support comprehension.	**RF.4.4:** Read with sufficient accuracy and fluency to support comprehension.	**RF.5.4:** Read with sufficient accuracy and fluency to support comprehension.
a. Read on-level text with purpose and understanding.	a. Read on-level text with purpose and understanding.	a. Read on-level text with purpose and understanding.
b. Read on-level prose and poetry orally with accuracy, appropriate rate, and expression on successive readings.	b. Read on-level prose and poetry orally with accuracy, appropriate rate, and expression on successive readings.	b. Read on-level prose and poetry orally with accuracy, appropriate rate, and expression on successive readings.
c. Use context to confirm or self-correct word recognition and understanding, re-reading as necessary.	c. Use context to confirm or self-correct word recognition and understanding, re-reading as necessary.	c. Use context to confirm or self-correct word recognition and understanding, re-reading as necessary.

Source: Adapted from NGA & CCSSO, 2010a, p. 17.

Fourth-grade teacher Meghan Forrester uses readers' theatre to gain a sense of her students' word-recognition skills and fluency. They perform excerpts of *Harriet the Spy* (Fitzhugh, 1964) because there is so much dialogue and because the humor is often best appreciated through the characters' words.

"At 780 Lexile, it's at the lower end of the grade band. Plus, qualitatively it's pretty straightforward. The students know a lot about the genre of a realistic fiction, and the content isn't very convoluted," Ms. Forrester offers. "It gives us a good place to start in the first month of school as I get to know them as readers. It also allows me to assess their fluency and determine where I need to go with my instruction."

Using scripts the fourth-grade collaborative team developed, students read and practice scenes for their Friday performances. "We call ourselves the Panther Players," Ms. Forrester notes, alluding to the school's mascot. Small groups each perform a different scene from the chapters read during the week, and she provides time for them each day to work on the script (Martinez, Roser, & Strecker, 1999). As students meet to assign roles, practice, and discuss the scripts, Ms. Forrester assesses each student's ability to read with fluency and prosody. "I really like listening to them on the first day, because I get a real sense of how they approach a word they don't know," Ms. Forrester says. "It takes me a few weeks to get an assessment on each student, but I find it's time well spent. I know what I need to teach, and to whom. And there's nothing wrong with the added benefit of boosting their understanding of the story, too!"

Conclusion

The Common Core State Standards for reading build on content teachers already know. Students in grades 3–5 still need instruction in the foundational skills of reading, as well as how to read narrative and expository texts. But the Common Core for English language arts require that teachers raise their expectations and provide students with access to complex texts and scaffolded instruction to justify their ideas and opinions. To ensure that students are prepared to meet these increased expectations, teachers have to plan new lessons that allow students to consolidate their understanding and apply what they have learned. This is a tall order for an individual teacher. But when teachers work in collaborative teams within a professional learning community to plan instruction and review student performance, creating new lessons is possible and enjoyable. As we have noted throughout this chapter, collaborative teams should focus their planning conversations around four questions:

1. What is familiar in the CCSS at each grade level?

2. What appears to be new based on prior standards?

3. What may be challenging for students?

4. What may be challenging for teachers?

In addition, collaborative teams should engage in lesson planning and a systematic review of student performance to determine which lessons are effective for which students, and what they need to do to ensure that all students reach the standard. We will focus on common formative assessment and responding to students who do not meet the expectations during initial instruction in the final chapter of this book. Before doing so, we will explore the Common Core standards for writing, speaking and listening, and language.

CHAPTER 3

Implementing the Common Core State Standards for Writing

KEY QUESTIONS

- To what extent does your team understand the Writing standards: What is the essence of each standard? What teacher actions facilitate the standards in practice? What evidence will we accept that students are learning the standards?

- How do the three major text types influence the writing assignments students complete and the genres they must learn?

- How is technology used to allow students to produce and publish their writing such that they can interact and collaborate with others?

The students in Helena Armendariz's fifth-grade science classroom have been exploring the topic of oceans for several weeks. They live in a state with nearly 1,000 miles of coastline, and the ocean plays a vital role in their local community. But even though their neighborhood is less than ten miles away from the beach, most of her students have never seen the sea.

Knowing that economic circumstances and cultural practices have limited her students' experiences on this topic, Ms. Armendariz coordinates a scientific expedition to study the tide pools in a nearby community. She works with a local university's oceanographic institute to prepare her students for the experience, and the class reads numerous informational books, articles, and even the institute's website to build background knowledge. Together she and the students create a plan to study the intertidal ecosystem and gather data (like population, species size, and location) on three assigned species from a list of those the institute's scientists are monitoring. The next day, Ms. Armendariz's junior scientists (as they now call themselves) meet in lab groups to analyze their data and write a report of their findings to the institute. Using the format for a scientific report, each group composes a joint report that includes an introduction to the project, a summary of the research on intertidal zones from their unit studies, a statement of the purpose of their expedition, the procedures they used to gather the data, their results, and a conclusion. To refine the report, each group meets with another to read and comment on the drafts.

Benito's group studies acorn barnacles, common rockweed, and California mussels. He and his group members assemble the digital photographs they took and the measurements, number, and location of each species they found, using a grid system the institute uses. Over the next week, Benito and his other group members compose the report using an online wiki document, allowing members to revise collaboratively.

Ms. Armendariz views each group's progress and gauges individual member's contributions. "It wouldn't be useful for the oceanographic institute to get thirty-three separate reports from my students," she says. "This collaborative writing really mirrored what they did to gather the data and analyze it. Writing is not always solitary. In science, you're often writing with your colleagues."

A Collaborative Planning Team in Action

The genesis for Ms. Armendariz's oceanography unit came from collaborative conversations with her fellow team members in grades 3–5. After their analysis of the Common Core State Standards for writing, they identified several goals for improvement in their writing instruction. Scientific writing was at the top of their list.

She notes, "We realized that while we were teaching about science using an inquiry model, our students didn't do much with writing. Most writing they did was about their personal experiences, and rarely was it related to any content areas other than language arts."

Noting that the CCSS for writing prominently featured informational and explanatory texts, these teachers develop a cohesive strand for science writing throughout the grades.

"By the time they get to fifth grade, we want them to be familiar with how you organize your thoughts and your data in a more formal way," Ms. Armendariz states. "We have an obligation to prepare students for writing in middle school, and our hope is that these collaborative writing experiences strengthen their ability to write scientific reports like this independently."

In chapter 2, we introduced four questions for the collaborative team to use when analyzing and discussing the Common Core Reading standards: What's new? What's familiar? What may be challenging for students? What may be challenging for teachers? Collaborative teams may decide to continue using those questions as they investigate the writing standards. However, we propose a different tool to analyze the writing standards, one that can facilitate discussion about the links between (1) standards, (2) instruction, and (3) formative assessment.

1. **Standards:** What is the essence of this standard?

2. **Instruction:** What teacher actions facilitate this standard in practice?

3. **Formative assessment:** What evidence will we accept that students are learning this standard?

Ms. Armendariz's collaborative team uses a similar method when first unpacking the writing standards. Figure 3.1 is a protocol for conducting this inquiry.

Writing anchor standard six (W.CCR.6): Use technology, including the Internet, to produce and publish writing and to interact and collaborate with others.

CCSS grade band: Grades 3–5

Anchor standard domain: Production and Distribution of Writing

Grade-Level Standard	Standard: What Is the Essence of This Standard?	Instruction: What Teacher Actions Facilitate This Standard in Practice?	Formative Assessment: What Evidence Will We Accept That Students Are Learning This Standard?
Grade 3 **W.3.6:** With guidance and support from adults, use technology to produce and publish writing, as well as to interact and collaborate with others.			
Grade 4 **W.4.6:** With some guidance and support from adults, use technology, including the Internet, to produce and publish writing as well as to interact and collaborate with others; demonstrate sufficient command of keyboarding skills to type a minimum of one page in a single sitting.			
Grade 5 **W.5.6:** With some guidance and support from adults, use technology, including the Internet, to produce and publish writing as well as to interact and collaborate with others; demonstrate sufficient command of keyboarding to type a minimum of two pages in a single sitting.			

Source: Adapted from NGA & CCSSO, 2010a, p. 21.

Figure 3.1: Guiding questions for grade-by-grade analysis of the Writing standards.

Visit go.solution-tree.com/commoncore for a reproducible version of this figure.

Anchor Standards for Writing

The college and career readiness anchor standards for writing were designed to articulate the need for a strong foundation across disciplines, audiences, and purposes. Writing, like speaking, is a form of communication. However, two important differences exist with writing: the audience is often unseen, and the product is often permanent. The fact is that we judge others by what they write and how they say it. Too many misspellings and we wonder whether the person is careless. We assume disorganized discourse is the product of a jumbled mind. We often dismiss opinions altogether if there is nothing to back up the claims. In each case, the writer may be careful, organized, and articulate, but writing may fail him or her. The anchor standards are an effort to ensure that students are able to communicate effectively in written form in order to represent themselves in the classroom, workplace, and world. There are ten anchor standards for writing, extending from kindergarten through twelfth grade. These standards are further organized into four domains: Text Types and Purposes, Production and Distribution of Writing, Research to Build and Present Knowledge, and Range of Writing (see NGA & CCSSO, 2010a, p. 8).

Text Types and Purposes

This domain has three anchor standards (W.CCR.1, 2, and 3) which define three major types of writing that are tied to their purposes—writing for argumentation, writing to inform or explain, and writing to convey real or imagined experiences. These basic text types are expressed through many writing genres, which in themselves are often a blend of two or more text types. For example, an opinion piece may include elements of argument, as well as narrative to describe the writer's perspective. Therefore, these should not be viewed too narrowly as a mandate to teach only three writing genres. Rather, it is an important reminder to us as educators that we need to clearly link purposes for writing, not just the format for a genre.

1. Write arguments to support claims in an analysis of substantive topics or texts, using valid reasoning and relevant and sufficient evidence. (W.CCR.1)

2. Write informative/explanatory texts to examine and convey complex ideas and information clearly and accurately through the effective selection, organization, and analysis of content. (W.CCR.2)

3. Write narratives to develop real or imagined experiences or events using effective technique, well-chosen details, and well-structured event sequences. (W.CCR.3) (NGA & CCSSO, 2010a, p. 8)

Production and Distribution of Writing

This domain focuses on the communicative nature of writing. Anchor standard four (W.CCR.4) encourages us to link the task, purpose, and audience to the selected genre or format. In anchor standard six (W.CCR.6), we can see how writing is lifted from a solitary and isolated act to one that involves peers, fellow writers, teachers, and experts across the classroom, community, and world. Anchor standard five (W.CCR.5) bridges the other two standards in this domain, articulating the processes a writer must necessarily engage with in order to communicate effectively.

4. Produce clear and coherent writing in which the development, organization, and style are appropriate to task, purpose, and audience. (W.CCR.4)

5. Develop and strengthen writing as needed by planning, revising, editing, rewriting, or trying a new approach. (W.CCR.5)

6. Use technology, including the Internet, to produce and publish writing and to interact and collaborate with others. (W.CCR.6) (NGA & CCSSO, 2010a, p. 8)

Research to Build and Present Knowledge

The importance of academic writing is foregrounded in this domain, which has three anchor standards (W.CCR.7, 8, and 9). Learners are encouraged to gather information from a variety of sources in order to investigate topics of worth. These should be a natural extension of the learning students engage in across their academic career—not just as consumers of information, but also as users and producers of the same. This requires that they critically analyze information sources, both literary and informational, and use it in their writing to conduct inquiry and research.

7. Conduct short as well as more sustained research projects based on focused questions, demonstrating understanding of the subject under investigation. (W.CCR.7)

8. Gather relevant information from multiple print and digital sources, assess the credibility and accuracy of each source, and integrate the information while avoiding plagiarism. (W.CCR.8)

9. Draw evidence from literary or informational texts to support analysis, reflection, and research. (W.CCR.9) (NGA & CCSSO, 2010a, p. 8)

Range of Writing

The key word in anchor standard ten (W.CCR.10) is *routinely*—writing is not something that is done only occasionally, but daily, and for extended periods of time in order to increase volume. As with reading, the intent is to build skill and stamina through frequent application and practice. This is a notable departure from the practices of many upper-elementary teachers. Gilbert and Graham's (2010) national survey of teachers in grades 4–6 finds that only fifteen minutes a day are devoted to writing instruction, compared to forty minutes a day in primary grades. In addition, grades 4–6 students spend only twenty-five minutes a day producing writing of a paragraph or more in length. As the authors note, writing instruction truly is "the prisoner of time" (Gilbert & Graham, 2010, p. 511).

10. Write routinely over extended time frames (time for research, reflection, and revision) and shorter time frames (a single sitting or a day or two) for a range of tasks, purposes, and audiences. (W.CCR.10) (NGA & CCSSO, 2010a, p. 8)

The anchor standards frame a vision for writing across grades K–12. But before analyzing the standards for grades 3–5 in more detail, it is useful to gain a perspective on the development of writers from the primary grades to graduation. In understanding the behaviors of young writers, we can better interpret how these anchor standards link to grade-level expectations.

Characteristics of Writers

Classrooms are filled with students with different strengths and needs. In terms of writing, students in a given classroom do not all write equally well and do not all share the same instructional needs. As we have noted, however, the Common Core State Standards provide teachers with information about appropriate grade-level expectations for writing acumen. These standards reflect an understanding about writing development and growth through four stages: (1) emergent, (2) early, (3) transitional, and (4) self-extending. Although there is a correlation between a student's age and his or her stage of writing development, it is important to recognize the writing behaviors evident at each stage of development since classrooms are diverse places filled with students who have gaps in their experiences as well as extensive background knowledge. Table 3.1 describes characteristics for each writing stage.

Table 3.1: Characteristics of Writers

Emergent Writers . . .	Early Writers . . .
• Are learning how print works • See the permanence of writing • Retell events in sequence • Use simple sentence construction • Use known words prominently	• Have rapid recall of letters and known words • Will use formulaic writing • Have writing constrained by limited known words • Use story grammar • Write longer texts, although ideas may not be consistent
Transitional Writers . . .	**Self-Extending Writers . . .**
• Apply text structures in their original writing • Recognize audience • Write longer texts with sustained ideas • Use more complex sentences • Use transition phrases and conjunctions	• Communicate a purposeful direction to audience • See writing as an extension of the writer • Write in multiple genres • Use words that are sophisticated and flexible • Engage in all aspects of editing

Visit **go.solution-tree.com/commoncore** for a reproducible version of this table.

Emergent Writers

These writers are just beginning to gain control of print and how it works. They are still learning that print carries a message and that they can create a new idea and then represent it on paper for others to appreciate. Emergent writers can generate text that retells a sequence of events in a story or in their personal lives, although the language used is likely to be fairly simple, with few complex sentences containing more than one or two ideas. Their writing contains letters and words they know, and their name is likely to be prominently featured in their texts. Emergent writers:

- Learn how print works including spaces and punctuation

- Develop an understanding that their ideas can be written and re-read

- Integrate their ideas with known words

Early Writers

Early writers are able to more rapidly recall letters, and therefore can scribe their message more quickly. However, they are prone to formulaic writing that incorporates the limited number of words they can spell. (Any first-grade teacher can testify to the plethora of student-generated sentences that begin with "I like"). These early writers are engaging in editing, as evidenced by the increase in eraser marks and crossed-out words. They can generate their own ideas for writing topics and are applying some elements of story grammar, such as character, setting, plot, and problem and solution to their own writing. Later in this phase, students will begin writing multiparagraph texts, although the ideas introduced at the beginning of the piece may get lost along the way. Early writers:

- Increase their writing speed and accuracy

- Produce longer pieces of text, although they often lose the thread of their ideas

- Generate their own stories with increasingly complex plots and characters

Transitional Writers

Students in this phase of development are actively incorporating varied approaches in their original writing. For example, they create titles for their pieces, use *grabber* sentences to gain the reader's attention, and use descriptive vocabulary to evoke a response from the reader. Indeed, recognizing the role of the audience is a hallmark of the writers in this phase of development. They are beginning to apply rudimentary structures to longer texts, such as listing directions for completing a task or writing a biography that contains the type of information expected in this literary form. Because their vocabulary has grown along with their sophistication of the language, more complex sentences containing multiple idea units are evident. Students at this stage can utilize transition phrases and conjunctions to build these longer sentences. Their stamina has increased as well. Both mean sentence length and overall length of the text has increased. An important indicator of a transitional writer is his or her ability to sustain an idea or concept over the course of multiple paragraphs.

Students in the transitional phase of writing are engaged in using a wide range of genres in their writing. They can write short informational reports using academic vocabulary, create multiparagraph essays on personal experiences, and construct original poems. They use conventional spelling and grammatical structures but often confuse irregular forms of words or grammar (for example, *gooses* instead of *geese*; *have went* instead of *have gone*). They use compound sentences.

Although this phase, like the others, is not strictly bound by grade level, many transitional writers emerge between grades 3–5. These transitional writers are more cognizant of the processes associated with writing. They are revising more of their work based on feedback from peers and the teacher, although this is more likely to be at the sentence and paragraph level rather than the document level. They are becoming more sophisticated in their use of multiple sources of information to support their own writing. Transitional writers:

- Write in multiple genres (for example, poetry, informational reports, narratives, and persuasive essays)

- Engage in author studies to examine the craft of writing (for example, an author study of Daniel Handler to learn irony or Christopher Paul Curtis to learn dialogue)

- Write rules and procedures for a variety of activities to practice technical writing (for example, directions for how to travel from school to the student's home)

- Create persuasive pieces to support a position (for example, "Why I should have a pet")

Self-Extending Writers

These sophisticated writers understand they are engaged in a complex process that is influenced by their application of specific strategies. This metacognitive awareness serves them well in being able to analyze their own writing as well as the writing of others. Self-extending writers are expanding their repertoire of writing genres and can write narratives, persuasive essays, technical documents, responses to literature, and biographies and autobiographies. Importantly, they understand that each of these genres has specific rules; the skills used to create a science lab report differ from writing a poem. Their control of the language, especially as it applies to vocabulary and multiple meanings, makes it easier for them to engage in a full editing process.

Students in this writing phase are notable for their ability to select the appropriate genre to match the task. They are learning to organize their ideas for longer pieces so that the plot moves well (for narrative) or the information is described in a logical manner (for expository). They increasingly use more complex sentences, and their word choice becomes more precise. Self-extending writers work toward two ideals: concise and precise. Their ability to edit is more sophisticated, and they are more likely to re-read their writing and retool sentences or sections to more clearly support subsequent text. Self-extending writers:

- Operate flexibly between genres (that is, they can develop multiple forms of writing during the same day)

- Seek peer and teacher feedback and integrate it into their writing

- Recognize the value of using wide variety of sources to develop their writing and seek original sources, not just those the teacher provides

- Use accurate and innovative punctuation, word usage, and grammatical structures

- Demonstrate individual voice and style

- Utilize writing as a means of clarifying their own thinking

Samples of Student Writing

Observing how students are developing as writers is an important aspect of teaching writing well. The Common Core ELA contains a collection of student writing examples that will enable you and your collaborative team to gain added insights into what student writing looks like at various stages. As a future task for your team, use the student writing examples for grades 3–5 featured in appendix C (NGA & CCSSO, 2010d). Collectively, these examples reflect a range of writing ability and were constructed under several conditions, including on-demand writing, as well as more polished pieces that were developed through several rounds of editing and revision. These include a narrative piece and an informative and explanatory sample at all three grade levels, as well as opinions pieces in grades 4 and 5. We encourage your collaborative team to examine these together across the grade band in order to gain a better sense of the progression to look for with transitional writers. These samples can serve as anchor papers for developing a consensus scoring procedure to be used at each grade level. These consensus scoring events serve as a fine-tuning process for educators and provide valuable formative assessment data for making instructional decisions.

As we have noted previously, the Common Core State Standards articulate expectations for students across grade levels based on a common set of anchor standards. We'll explore the specific writing standards for grades 3–5 in the following section.

Writing Standards for Grades 3–5

The grade-level standards for writing are organized in the same manner as the anchor standards they are derived from: Text Types and Purposes, Production and Distribution of Writing, Research to Build and Present Knowledge, and Range of Writing (NGA &

CCSSO, 2010a). We hope that teachers meet in their collaborative team to discuss these standards using the protocol introduced at the beginning of this chapter.

1. **Standards:** What is the essence of this standard?

2. **Instruction:** What teacher actions facilitate this standard in practice?

3. **Formative assessment:** What evidence will we accept that students are learning this standard?

Text Types and Purposes

The first three standards in this domain define three basic text types used in and out of school—(1) opinion, (2) informative and explanatory, and (3) narrative (see table 3.2, page 71). Although the anchor standard calls the first type *argument*, the NGA and CCSSO (2010b) acknowledge that young writers are not yet developmentally situated to write for formal arguments:

> They develop a variety of methods to extend and elaborate their work by providing examples, offering reasons for their assertions, and explaining cause and effect. These kinds of expository structures are steps on the road to argument. (p. 23)

The three standards parallel one another, with third grade's emphasis on using linking words and phrases, as well as signal words, to organize information and stories. By fourth grade, students are adding more formal writing features, such as using quotations, headings, and concluding statements. The fifth-grade level expectations are identical, as these writing behaviors require extended practice and experiences.

As stated earlier in this chapter, text *type* should not be confused with writing *genre*. Students will encounter a multitude of genres in their literate lives. Specifically what constitutes a genre has been debated, but most people agree that there should be similarities in form, style, or subject matter for something to be called a genre (Coker, 2007; Kress, 1999; Miller, 1984; Short, Schroeder, Kauffman, & Kaser, 2004; Turbill & Bean, 2006). In other words, a genre has defining characteristics that are unique to a group of works. The genres students read may not be the genres that they learn to write, at least at grades 3–5. For example, students may read westerns, science fiction, horror, fantasy, realistic fiction, poetry, and a host of other genres.

The Common Core State Standards identify three major text types: (1) opinion and persuasive, (2) informative and explanatory, and (3) narrative (NGA & CCSSO, 2010b). For each text type, there are specific genres that students should know and be able to use. Students are taught the characteristics of these genres so they can use these elements in their own writing. Skillful use of these elements allows the writer to convey ideas in a way that the intended audience understands. Table 3.3 (page 74) contains a summary of common features of each text type and its genres, features, and writing characteristics.

Table 3.2: Writing Standards for Domain Text Types and Purposes, Grades 3–5

Anchor Standards	Grade 3 Standards	Grade 4 Standards	Grade 5 Standards
W.CCR.1: Write arguments to support claims in an analysis of substantive topics or texts, using valid reasoning and relevant and sufficient evidence.	**W.3.1:** Write opinion pieces on topics or texts, supporting a point of view with reasons. a. Introduce the topic or text they are writing about, state an opinion, and create an organizational structure that lists reasons. b. Provide reasons that support the opinion. c. Use linking words and phrases (like because, therefore, since, and for example) to connect opinion and reasons. d. Provide a concluding statement or section.	**W.4.1:** Write opinion pieces on topics or texts, supporting a point of view with reasons and information. a. Introduce a topic or text clearly, state an opinion, and create an organizational structure in which related ideas are grouped to support the writer's purpose. b. Provide reasons that are supported by facts and details. c. Link opinion and reasons using words and phrases (like for instance, in order to, and in addition). d. Provide a concluding statement or section related to the opinion presented.	**W.5.1:** Write opinion pieces on topics or texts, supporting a point of view with reasons and information. a. Introduce a topic or text clearly, state an opinion, and create an organizational structure in which ideas are logically grouped to support the writer's purpose. b. Provide logically ordered reasons that facts and details support. c. Link opinion and reasons using words, phrases, and clauses (like consequently and specifically). d. Provide a concluding statement or section related to the opinion presented.
W.CCR.2: Write informative and explanatory texts to examine and convey complex ideas and information clearly and accurately through the effective selection, organization, and analysis of content.	**W.3.2:** Write informative and explanatory texts to examine a topic and convey ideas and information clearly.	**W.4.2:** Write informative and explanatory texts to examine a topic and convey ideas and information clearly.	**W.5.2:** Write informative and explanatory texts to examine a topic and convey ideas and information clearly.

continued →

Anchor Standards	Grade 3 Standards	Grade 4 Standards	Grade 5 Standards
W.CCR.2: Write informative and explanatcry texts to examine and convey complex ideas and information clearly and accurately through the effective selection, organization, and analysis of content.	a. Introduce a topic and group related information together; include illustrations when useful to aiding comprehension. b. Develop the topic with facts, definitions, and details. c. Use linking words and phrases (like also, another, and, more, and but) to connect ideas within categories of information. d. Provide a concluding statement or section.	a. Introduce a topic clearly and group related information in paragraphs and sections; include formatting (like headings), illustrations, and multimedia when useful to aiding comprehension. b. Develop the topic with facts, definitions, concrete details, quotations, or other information and examples related to the topic. c. Link ideas within categories of information using words and phrases (like another, for example, also, and because). d. Use precise language and domain-specific vocabulary to inform about or explain the topic. e. Provide a concluding statement or section related to the information or explanation presented.	a. Introduce a topic clearly, provide a general observation and focus, and group related information logically; include formatting (like headings), illustrations, and multimedia when useful to aiding comprehension. b. Develop the topic with facts, definitions, concrete details, quotations, or other information and examples related to the topic. c. Link ideas within and across categories of information using words, phrases, and clauses (like in contrast and especially). d. Use precise language and domain-specific vocabulary to inform about or explain the topic. e. Provide a concluding statement or section related to the information or explanation presented.

W.CCR.3: Write narratives to develop real or imagined experiences or events using effective technique, well-chosen details and well-constructed event sequences.	**W.3.3:** Write narratives to develop real or imagined experiences or events using effective technique, descriptive details, and clear event sequences.	**W.4.3:** Write narratives to develop real or imagined experiences or events using effective technique, descriptive details, and clear event sequences.	**W.5.3:** Write narratives to develop real or imagined experiences or events using effective technique, descriptive details, and clear event sequences.
	a. Establish a situation and introduce a narrator or characters; organize an event sequence that unfolds naturally.	a. Orient the reader by establishing a situation and introducing a narrator or characters; organize an event sequence that unfolds naturally.	a. Orient the reader by establishing a situation and introducing a narrator or characters; organize an event sequence that unfolds naturally.
	b. Use dialogue and descriptions of actions, thoughts, and feelings to develop experiences and events or show the response of characters to situations.	b. Use dialogue and description to develop experiences and events or show the responses of characters to situations.	b. Use narrative techniques, such as dialogue, description, and pacing, to develop experiences and events or show the responses of characters to situations.
	c. Use temporal words and phrases to signal event order.	c. Use a variety of transitional words and phrases to manage the sequence of events.	c. Use a variety of transitional words, phrases, and clauses to manage the sequence of events.
	d. Provide a sense of closure.	d. Use concrete words and phrases and sensory details to convey experiences and events precisely.	d. Use concrete words and phrases and sensory details to convey experiences and events precisely.
		e. Provide a conclusion that follows from the narrated experiences or events.	e. Provide a conclusion that follows from the narrated experiences or events.

Source: Adapted from NGA & CCSSO, 2010a, pp. 18 and 21.

Table 3.3: CCSS Text Types and Genres

Text Type	Genres	Features	Writing Characteristics
Opinion and Persuasive	Essays, speeches, editorials, and letters to the editor	States an opinion or point of view and provide reasons and information Seeks to convince a reader about the validity of a position or action	Define a position. Offer supporting evidence using primary and secondary sources. Address concerns of the reader.
Informative and Explanatory	Report of information, summary, and technical analysis and literary analysis	Conveys factual reports containing information or observations Briefly restates a text's main ideas Presents instructions and procedures	Use multiple sources and document sources. Refrain from expressing opinions. Identify sequence accurately. Use correct format for document.
Narrative	Autobiography biography, creative fiction, and memoirs	Uses time as a deep structure Has a narrator Establishes a situation and sequence	Inform, instruct, persuade, or entertain. Use monologue or dialogue, visual details, and actions.

Source: Adapted from NGA & CCSSO, 2010b, pp. 23–24.

Opinion and Persuasive Writing

Everyone has an opinion but not everyone can support his or her opinion with reasons and information. Furthermore, not everyone can share his or her opinion in ways that encourage discussion about different viewpoints or the use of persuasive techniques to convince others about the argument. As students learn to share their opinions with others, they develop persuasive abilities. In opinion pieces and persuasive writing, students must support their points of view and eventually, even if not fully developed in grades 3–5, try to convince others to agree with the facts as they present them, share values that are outlined, accept specific argument and conclusions, or adopt a way of thinking. This type of writing is often regarded as the most difficult for students to master. Students must commit to a line of reasoning and not introduce new topics within the paper. In addition, they need to demonstrate clear thinking through convincing arguments, and support those statements with ample, credible evidence. At the end of the piece, they must summarize their logic and thinking as a conclusion.

Informational and Explanatory Writing

A *factual report* conveys information or observations, often generically referred to as an *essay*. The purpose of this type of writing is to inform, not to persuade or react. It is commonly used in science and social studies contexts. Students must learn not to interject themselves or their opinions into this type of writing and instead use credible sources to support the facts they present. Typically, a factual report has a common structure that includes an opening paragraph that explains to readers what they will find in the paper, the body that leads readers through the pertinent information, and a conclusion that summarizes the report's information. In other words, an informative or explanatory piece provides a forum for writers to report the information they have analyzed, summarize conclusions they have drawn from the information, consider alternatives to the information presented, and make a series of recommendations based on the information.

Narrative Writing

Students are also expected to write accounts of their lives and the lives of others, real or imagined. In our experience, students particularly like this text type. They enjoy reading about others and take pleasure in writing about themselves and people they find interesting. The key to writing good narratives is to collect enough information to tell a good story about the person, event, or experience. Students should learn to use descriptive language to capture the readers' interest and employ a variety of narrative techniques such as story grammar, dialogue, and literary devices. As students get older and become more skilled writers, they will be asked to produce papers in which they analyze a piece of literature or a poem. Typically a series of questions guide their writing, such as:

- What happened in the story?

- What point do you think the author is making in the story?

- Do you think the story mirrors real life?

To respond to these types of questions, students need experience writing these responses, talking about literature, and receiving feedback.

Fifth-grade social studies teacher Aida Allen's students meet with her to receive instruction about writing an explanatory piece based on a text they have read. Ms. Allen distributes a reading that she will be using for the next few lessons—*They Fought for Freedom: Children in the Civil Rights Movement* (Feldman, 1999). This sixteen-page expository text is part of the school's fifth-grade social studies collection and covers content related to the social studies standards. Ms. Allen asks the students to read silently for a few minutes and motions for Leo to *whisper read* so she can listen. She writes some anecdotal notes about Leo's performance in her notebook so that she can share this student's progress at her collaborative team meeting later that afternoon. After a couple of minutes, Ms. Allen invites the students to turn their attention back to her.

Because the book offers so many photographs, she asks the students to review them and make a prediction about when it took place. Anahi immediately remarks that one photograph "looks like the kids in the movie *Grease*," and Bianca accurately predicts that the pictures were taken in the 1950s and 1960s. Robert locates both Rosa Parks and Martin Luther King Jr. in two other photographs. Ms. Allen uses a map of the United States to pinpoint several locations in the American South, and then points to the title of the book. Together, they discuss the focus of the informational text, which recounts the stories of six children who chose to act in heroic ways. They make connections with the class investigation of individuals who made a difference, and discuss the topic of investigation: How Freedom Was Won.

Ms. Allen predicts that her students will struggle with some key terms and wants to spend some time focused on *freedom*, *civil rights movement*, and *heroic*. As the students enter these words into their journals, she asks them about each word, building on their prior knowledge. She even points out the *-ic* suffix on *heroic* and connects it to other words on the word wall, including *fantastic* and *athletic*. She then distributes a graphic organizer (see figure 3.2) they will use to take notes about each of the children the book profiles.

Gwendolyn Patton	Ernest Green	Claudette Colvin
Age: 9	**Age:** 17	**Age:** 10
Year: 1950 and 1960	**Year:** 1957	**Year:** 1955
Heroic act: She dumped out her water on the counter in protest when they told her she could not sit there.	**Heroic act:** He was the first African American to graduate from an all-white school.	**Heroic act:** She refused to give up her seat to a white person on a bus.
Audrey Faye Hendricks	**Larry Russell**	**Sheyann Webb**
Age: 9	**Age:** 13–17	**Age:** 8
Year: 1963	**Year:** 1963	**Year:** 1965
Heroic act: She was in a protest march and was arrested. She was held for seven days.	**Heroic act:** He marched in the Children's Crusade and was arrested. He was held for ten days.	**Heroic act:** She was the youngest marcher in "Bloody Sunday" when the police attacked with clubs and tear gas.

Figure 3.2: Anahi's completed graphic organizer for *They Fought for Freedom*.

Ms. Allen turns the reading over to them again, asking them to read silently until they reach the bottom of the first profile on Gwendolyn Patton. After checking for understanding, she has them read silently to the end of the second profile. As the students read, she moves around the table, listening to the whisper reading of Bianca and Robert. As students finish reading, they begin to make notes on the graphic organizer. With a few minutes left in the lesson, Ms. Allen asks them to turn to a partner to tell one another about Gwendolyn's heroism. She partners with Anahi to hear her response. Finally, she asks whether the students thought Gwendolyn's actions helped or hurt the civil rights movement. Bianca answers in the affirmative, explaining that having a child sent away from a lunch counter would cause lots of people to be upset and talk about it.

Before the timer sounds, Ms. Allen asks the students to use the book to complete the graphic organizer section on Ernest Green, the second student profile they read. She circulates around the classroom, reading over students' shoulders to check their work. She reminds them that they should read the rest of the text independently, taking notes on each of the people they meet before they begin writing their factual report.

Figure 3.2 shows Anahi's completed graphic organizer. She is well on her way to responding to the question "How did these six children stand up for their rights," using evidence from the text to discuss the actions of various individuals during the civil rights movement to win freedom.

The start of Anahi's paper for the unit How Freedom Was Won suggests her developing understanding of the topic and her skills as a writer:

> Freedom is not something that other people give you. You have to earn it. This takes time and people who are willing to go against the rules. Earning freedom is not being rude, but it does require that people protest the actions of other people when they are not being treated fairly. In this paper, I will explain the life of three people who made a difference in the civil rights movement and how their actions helped people gain freedom.

Production and Distribution of Writing

This domain describes the procedural and technical aspects of writing (NGA & CCSSO, 2010a). Anchor standard four (W.CCR.4) stresses the importance of organization and its effect on coherence in writing, and relates much of this back to standards one to three in the domain Text Types and Purposes discussed in the previous section. Anchor standard five (W.CCR.5) foregrounds writing as a public and collaborative set of processes that require oral and written communicative skills, and refers further to the Language standards as they relate to grammar and conventions of standard English (these will be more fully explored in the next chapter). Finally, anchor standard six (W.CCR.6) extends the groundwork laid in the previous standard by defining the public space beyond the classroom and into digital environments. Table 3.4 (page 78) presents the anchor standards and grade-level standards. These standards represent a shift in how writing is taught. The technical skills of keyboarding and word processing need to be viewed as basic skills, in the same way that we view holding a pencil correctly. Sure, it's important for a time, but it's not our endpoint. No one would confuse pencil grip with written communication; we should not confound operating a word-processing program with writing, either.

Table 3.4: Writing Standards for Domain Production and Distribution of Writing, Grades 3–5

Anchor Standards	Grade 3 Standards	Grade 4 Standards	Grade 5 Standards
W.CCR.4: Produce clear and coherent writing in which the development, organization, and style are appropriate to task, purpose, and audience.	**W.3.4:** With guidance and support from adults, produce writing in which the development and organization are appropriate to task and purpose. (Grade-specific expectations for writing types are defined in standards one to three.)	**W.4.4:** Produce clear and coherent writing in which the development and organization are appropriate to task, purpose, and audience. (Grade-specific expectations for writing types are defined in standards one to three.)	**W.5.4:** Produce clear and coherent writing in which the development and organization are appropriate to task, purpose, and audience. (Grade-specific expectations for writing types are defined in standards one to three.)
W.CCR.5: Develop and strengthen writing as needed by planning, revising, editing, rewriting, or trying a new approach.	**W.3.5:** With guidance and support from peers and adults, develop and strengthen writing as needed by planning, revising, and editing. (Editing for conventions should demonstrate command of Language standards one to three up to and including grade 3.)	**W.4.5:** With guidance and support from peers and adults, develop and strengthen writing as needed by planning, revising, and editing. (Editing for conventions should demonstrate command of Language standards one to three up to and including grade 4.)	**W.5.5:** With guidance and support from peers and adults, develop and strengthen writing as needed by planning, revising, editing, rewriting, or trying a new approach. (Editing for conventions should demonstrate command of Language standards one to three up to and including grade 5.)
W.CCR.6: Use technology, including the Internet, to produce and publish writing and to interact and collaborate with others.	**W.3.6:** With guidance and support from adults, use technology to produce and publish writing (using keyboarding skills) as well as to interact and collaborate with others.	**W.4.6:** With some guidance and support from adults, use technology, including the Internet, to produce and publish writing as well as to interact and collaborate with others; demonstrate sufficient command of keyboarding skills to type a minimum of one page in a single sitting.	**W.5.6:** With some guidance and support from adults, use technology, including the Internet, to produce and publish writing as well as to interact and collaborate with others; demonstrate sufficient command of keyboarding skills to type a minimum of two pages in a single sitting.

Source: Adapted from NGA & CCSSO, 2010a, pp. 18 and 21.

These first two domains of the anchor standards for writing—(1) Text Types and Purposes and (2) Production and Distribution of Writing—reset our vision of what writing should be. It's not the *tools* of writing as much as it is the *functions*: we find, use, produce, and share information (Frey, Fisher, & Gonzalez, 2010). Young writers will encounter tools we can't even imagine at this point in the history of the information era, but if sufficiently equipped with a deep understanding of the functions of writing, they can adopt these new tools more quickly and more fully. Molly Hutchinson's third-grade classroom regularly uses digital tools to explore these functions. For example, her students produce and share their writing using the digital storyboard website VoiceThread (www.voicethread.com).

"What I like about digital storyboards is that the students really need to think about multimedia, whether it's narrative, informative, or persuasive," she says.

For Ms. Hutchinson, the best feature is that other students can leave comments, ask questions, and add information through text boxes or audio recordings.

"As each subsequent child views a writer's production, the written and spoken commentary of previous viewers is also included. I tell my students that it's like looking at the fingerprints of people who were there before you. And it gives the writer a sense of what others understand or still have questions about."

The public and collaborative nature of writing requires that students see themselves as both readers and writers. They are readers of published works, of course, but they are also readers of each other's writing. In addition, writers need to understand the importance of audience in shaping their writing. As students write longer pieces they need to find out what a reader understands. This is consistent with the practices of professional writers, who seek the feedback of an editor to refine their work. Peer response allows students to come together as fellow writers to read each other's work and give constructive feedback. However, we offer several caveats to the use of peer response:

- The writer determines when he or she needs peer feedback.
- The teacher and students recognize that not all writing needs peer feedback.
- Teachers, not students, should offer feedback on the details of the piece.
- Students should provide feedback that is focused on a reader's needs and a writer's strategies.

These guidelines are useful reminders that the writer decides when he or she is ready for peer feedback. Few things are more dispiriting than receiving criticism about a piece the writer knows is not ready for review. This can serve to discourage the writer and prevent him or her from seeking such feedback in the future. Peer response functions best in a classroom environment that is conducive to communication and in which experimentation is expected and honored.

Some peer responses are less helpful than others. In particular, global praise does little to provide the writer with any feedback that might be useful. Additionally, feedback that only focuses on word- and sentence-level editing mirrors what the teacher often does and may not be welcome by fellow students. Rather, the purpose of seeking peer responses is not to have the work evaluated but to hear what a reader understood and where the reader became confused (Simmons, 2003).

Once teachers instruct students on the types of appropriate responses, students can use a simple peer response form to give back to the writer. It is helpful for writers to receive comments in writing so they have an idea of what to do next. It should also be noted that the teacher should review these peer comments in order to monitor whether students are offering helpful feedback. Figure 3.3 is an example of a peer response form.

Peer Response for Writing

Reader: _____ Writer: _____

Title: _____ Date: _____

What are the best things about this writing?

Retell the main ideas of the story using your own words.

What questions do you have for the writer so you can understand the story better?

What specific suggestions do you have for the writer to make the piece stronger?

Figure 3.3: Peer response feedback form.

Visit **go.solution-tree.com/commoncore** for a reproducible version of this figure.

Third graders Jesse and Ray settle into two small rocking chairs below a sign that reads "Writers at Work." Earlier, Jesse asked Ray to read a report he had written about spiders. After reading it and filling out a peer response form, Ray was ready to talk with his friend about the piece. He looked at the posters hanging nearby—"How Fellow Writers Talk" and "How Fellow Writers Listen"—to help with their conversation.

How Fellow Writers Talk

1. Tell your fellow writer what you liked best.
2. Retell the story or main ideas in your own words.
3. Ask questions about the parts you don't understand.
4. Give your fellow writer your good ideas about making it even better.
5. Thank the writer for sharing his or her writing with you.

How Fellow Writers Listen

1. Listen to the ideas your fellow writer offers.
2. Ask questions about ideas you don't understand.
3. Thank your fellow writer for reading your writing.
4. Use the ideas you like in your writing.

Visit **go.solution-tree.com/commoncore** for a reproducible version of these feature boxes.

"I liked reading about spiders because I like spiders, too," begins Ray. "It was interesting, and I liked the part about the wolf spider best. I was surprised that some of them can kill a toad!"

"I liked that part, too!" says Jesse, warming to the topic.

Ray continues, "I think the main ideas you wrote about were that spiders are good because they eat bad insects, and they are mostly not poisonous. Then you told about weird spiders like wolf spiders, black widows, and funnel-web spiders."

Jesse responds, "That's right. That's what my report's about. I want to draw pictures of them, too."

"Here's my question about your spider report. Do any of these spiders live here? I would like to know if they live here," Ray offers.

"The funnel-web spider doesn't live here," says Jesse, sounding a little disappointed. "It only lives in Australia. It's a deadly spider, too. Australia has all the cool stuff. They have box jellyfish, too. That's the most poisonous jellyfish in the world. Maybe you could add something about the funnel-web spider to your report."

"I can help you draw the pictures if you want. There's a cool spider book in the library."

Research to Build and Present Knowledge

Anchor standards seven, eight, and nine in this domain set students on a writing path they will use throughout the remainder of their school and work lives: the ability to report experiences and information (see table 3.5, page 82). Anchor standard seven (W.CCR.7) introduces short research projects to third graders, extending their introductory experiences with co-constructed inquiry-based projects in the primary grades. By fifth grade, students are using multiple sources of information to more formally investigate a topic, as Ms. Armendariz's fifth graders did in their intertidal unit described at the beginning of this chapter.

Anchor standard eight (W.CCR.8) highlights the importance of organizing information during research, especially in making useful notes that can be utilized during the writing process. A student's ability to take and organize notes is a significant predictor of success.

A Focus on Annotation and Note Taking

Over time, and with instruction, students not only use their notes for externally storing information but also for encoding their ideas. This builds comprehension and understanding of the content (Ganske, 1981). Note taking is also critical skill for college success (Pauk, 1974), so it's an important skill to master early on.

Edgar Allan Poe (1844/1988), an unapologetic note maker in the margins of texts, writes, "In the marginalia, too, we talk only to ourselves; we therefore talk freshly—boldly—originally—with abandonment—without conceit" (p. 7). In their seminal text *How to Read a Book*, Mortimer Adler and Charles Van Doren (1972) lay out a case for engaging in repeated readings with accompanying annotation:

Table 3.5: Writing Standards for Domain Research to Build and Present Knowledge, Grades 3–5

Anchor Standards	Grade 3 Standards	Grade 4 Standards	Grade 5 Standards
W.CCR.7 Conduct short as well as more sustained research projects based on focused questions, demonstrating understanding of the subject under investigation.	**W.3.7:** Conduct short research projects that build knowledge about a topic.	**W.4.7:** Conduct short research projects that build knowledge through investigation of different aspects of a topic.	**W.5.7:** Conduct short research projects that use several sources to build knowledge through investigation of different aspects of a topic.
W.CCR.8: Gather relevant information from multiple print and digital sources, assess the credibility and accuracy of each source, and integrate the information while avoiding plagiarism.	**W.3.8:** Recall information from experiences or gather information from print and digital sources; take brief notes on sources and sort evidence into provided categories.	**W.4.8:** Recall relevant information from experiences or gather relevant information from print and digital sources; take notes and categorize information, and provide a list of sources.	**W.5.8:** Recall relevant information from experiences or gather relevant information from print and digital sources; summarize or paraphrase information in notes and finished work, and provide a list of sources.
W.CCR.9: Draw evidence from literary or informational texts to support analysis, reflection, and research.	n/a	**W.4.9:** Draw evidence from literary or informational texts to support analysis, reflection, and research. a. Apply grade 4 Reading standards to literature (for example, "Describe in depth a character, setting, or event in a story or drama, drawing on specific details in the text [such as a character's thoughts, words, or actions]"). b. Apply grade 4 Reading standards to informational texts (for example, "Explain how an author uses reasons and evidence to support particular points in a text").	**W.5.9:** Draw evidence from literary or informational texts to support analysis, reflection, and research. a. Apply grade 5 Reading standards to literature (for example, "Compare and contrast two or more characters, settings, or events in a story or a drama, drawing on specific details in the text [such as how characters interact]"). b. Apply grade 5 Reading standards to informational texts (for example, "Explain how an author uses reasons and evidence to support particular points in a text, identifying which reasons and evidence support which points").

Source: Adapted from NGA & CCSSO, 2010a, pp. 18 and 21.

Why is marking a book indispensable to reading it? First, it keeps you awake—not merely conscious, but wide awake. Second, reading, if active, is thinking, and thinking tends to express itself in words, spoken or written. The person who says he knows what he thinks but cannot express it usually does not know what he thinks. Third, writing your reactions down helps you remember the thoughts of the author. (p. 49)

They go on to describe the most common annotation marks (Adler & Van Doren, 1940/1972):

- **Underlines** for major points

- **Vertical lines** in the margin for statements that are too long to be underlined

- **Star, asterisk, or other symbol** in the margin to emphasize the ten or twelve most important statements (folding the corner or bookmarking the page is a helpful way to quickly turn back to these)

- **Numbers** in the margin to indicate a sequence of points the author makes to develop an argument

- **Page numbers** in the margin to indicate where else the author makes the same points

- **Circles** for key words or phrases

- **Questions (and perhaps answers)** in the margin or at the top or bottom of the page that come to mind while reading

Additionally, Susan Vanneman (2011) suggests that note taking is as easy as ABC LOU, a mnemonic device that stands for *abbreviations*, *bullets*, *caveman language*, *lists*, *one word for several*, and *use your own words*. Using annotations and mnemonics are just a couple ways students can take quick but efficient notes.

However, the question remains, what kind of note-taking system works? As Jean Faber, John Morris, and Mary Lieberman (2000) find, the Cornell note-taking system increases comprehension (and test scores). Using this system, a piece of paper is divided into three sections: (1) the right side for notes and tasks, (2) the left side for questions and key points, and (3) the bottom for a summary. Key points help students quickly find information, locate references, and conduct research projects, which prepares students for W.CCR.10 (and W.CCR.9 in grades 6–12), "Draw evidence from literary or informational texts to support analysis, reflection, and research" (NGA & CCSSO, 2010a, p. 10).

Other Note-Taking Methods

Of course, there are other ways for students to take notes. In the primary grades, students can take group notes through interactive writing events (Frey & Fisher, 2007b). This may involve a group of students talking about a text and then sharing the pen to create their notes—using a Cornell format or a graphic organizer. As they get older, students can also learn to take notes digitally using laptops or tablets (Horney et al., 2009). Daniel Callison and Leslie Preddy (2006) identify four note-taking strategies for web pages: (1) highlight key terms and statements, (2) write a summary, (3) recite information learned, and (4) cite the source. The website NoteStar (http://notestar.4teachers.org) allows students to collect and organize their notes using some given fields that teachers create or assign.

Regardless of the format, students should learn the five Rs of note taking: (1) record meaningful facts and ideas; (2) reduce the text to main ideas and summaries; (3) recite the most important terms, concepts, ideas, and conclusions; (4) reflect on personal opinion and perspective; and (5) review. The key for teachers is to instruct students to extract meaningful information and record the sources.

Unlike the previous two, the last standard in this domain does not apply to third graders. Anchor standard nine (W.CCR.9) requires fourth- and fifth-grade writers to extract evidence, including direct quotes, in the literary and informational texts they read, in order to write about them. Again, this last standard in the domain may challenge teachers and their students, who may have grown accustomed to responding to, but not analyzing, the literature and informational texts they read. Stating that one likes (or does not like) a book doesn't especially challenge the writer to read deeply. Keep in mind that the reading standards call on students to read critically as they compare and contrast, describe problems and solutions, and so on. However, much of this critical analysis occurs when the writer has to put these ideas down on paper. Understanding follows action; it rarely precedes it. We come to understandings when we try things out, even when our initial attempts are unsuccessful. In order for readers to deeply understand text, they must write about it at a comparably complex level.

Writers invariably compose orally before they put their ideas into written form. These communicators carry critical-analysis skills from conversation into their writing. Discussion has great value across several dimensions. Discussions are an important source of information for learners, who can benefit from structures that give students an opportunity to formulate opinions, consider alternative views, and reach conclusions. An excellent technique for accomplishing all of these goals is the discussion web (Alvermann, 1991). A discussion web converges on a central question and is conducted in three distinct stages similar to the think-pair-share approach.

First, students write responses in favor of and opposed to a proposal. Then group members discuss their responses with one another. Next, they read a piece of text, looking for evidence defending both positions. Once again, the group discusses both sides of the issue, now utilizing evidence from the text to support the positions. After the discussion, the group members return to the discussion web to note any points they may have overlooked. Students now have an excellent tool to write an opinion piece for either position. This tool is especially useful because effective persuasion requires that the writer acknowledge the other side of the issue. See figure 3.4 for a sample discussion web.

Juan deCarlo's third-grade students construct a class discussion web during their social studies unit of study on community and change. A local historical site was slated for demolition to make way for a public plaza, until preservationists raised protests. The debate in the local community caught the attention of Mr. deCarlo, who saw this as an ideal topic for exploration by his students.

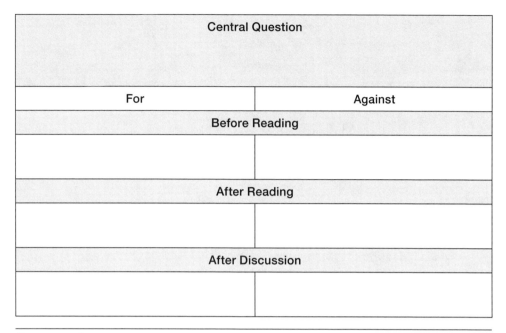

Figure 3.4: Sample discussion web.

Visit **go.solution-tree.com/commoncore** for a reproducible version of this figure.

"It was a way to have discussions about the common good, and to introduce the idea that most decisions are not wholly *good* or *bad*," he says. "I also saw this as a great way to get them to arrive at an informed opinion and then write about it."

Over the next week, his students compile evidence for both razing the old industrial building, as well as preserving it and restoring it to its former condition.

"We watched local news reports, and I read articles and editorials from the newspaper to the class," he says. "Each time, we'd add evidence supporting one plan or the other."

Mr. deCarlo often demonstrates how he took notes on the discussion web, stored electronically on his interactive whiteboard. When it came time to write a letter of support to the zoning board, students had a list of evidence to draw from.

"It was really interesting to see how they chose," he says. "It was about 50/50. I thought most of the kids would have just chosen the public plaza. After all, what do they care about an old building? But because we took the time to listen to both sides of the issue, they could see that the preservationists and the developers both had valid points."

As we will discuss in greater detail in chapter 4 on the strands Speaking and Listening and Language, paragraph frames can be used to guide students into academic writing. (See page 110.) Sentence frames can help students think about argumentation and evidence, as was the case when Mr. deCarlo provides his students with a number of sentence frames for their use, including:

- I agree/disagree with _____ because _____.

- They say _____ and/but I say _____ because _____.

- I agree with _____ (source) that _____ (opinion/perspective) because _____.

- From the perspective of _____, I think/understand _____.

Over time, these frames become part of students' writing habits and they use them automatically, while modifying the words to address the audience and topic (Fisher & Frey, 2007b). In her paper about saving the local historical site, Jasmine incorporates these sentence frames to make her point.

> *From the perspective of the preservationists, I understand that the building has a history that they want to share with people in the future. If the building is torn down, then babies born today will not get to see it and learn about the work that was done there to create the police department.*

In Javier Corrigan's fifth-grade classroom, students read *Hattie Big Sky* (Larson, 2006). As part of their collaborative team discussion, the teachers selected this book because it fits with their social studies content.

Mr. Corrigan notes, "The 700 Lexile score for this book is a little low for our grade but the content would be a bit of a stretch for third graders. After all, the main character is a sixteen-year-old orphan who moves to Montana by herself. Our team decided that the qualitative factors for this book, as well as the tasks we were going to ask of our students, made it appropriate for our unit of study. It's really a good choice for our overall investigation of westward expansion, human rights, and civil liberty."

Over the course of the investigation, students read from a number of primary-source documents and the historical-fiction text teachers selected. In doing so, they addressed a number of the Common Core State Standards. As we have noted previously, these standards lend themselves to integration, meaning that a given lesson may address several standards—for reading, writing, speaking and listening, and language—all at the same time. But the focus here is on writing. Mr. Corrigan and the other fifth-grade teachers in the collaborative planning team ensure that students could draw evidence from literary texts that support their analysis and research. To accomplish this, students write frequently in response to prompts that the collaborative team developed. Toward the end of the book, the teachers pose this question to the students: "Hattie nearly loses her homestead because of her age. Do you think Hattie ultimately lost her homestead because she was too young or for another reason?"

In his response, Jeremy focused on the newspaper article that Hattie wrote. His introduction focused on his response to the question, namely that Hattie did not lose her homestead due to her age. As part of his response, he included the following:

> *One piece of evidence that I offer in support of my position is the newspaper article that Hattie wrote in September 1918. She begins her article with "So much fuss about age!" (p. 244) and then gives several*

examples about how society has different rules for different ages. She even reminds readers that "sixteen-year-old boys are left in charge of farms while their fathers go east for work" (p. 245). I think that this is evidence from the characters own perspective that age was not the reason that she lost her homestead.

Another piece of evidence that supports my position is the weather during the time that Hattie was trying to save the homestead. Hattie was not the only person who had problems that year. As we read about in the almanac, there was really bad weather that caused a lot of people to lose their farms and homesteads. Hattie says, "The sky hurled hailstone after hailstone onto my field" (p. 239), which caused her a lot of problems with the crops. Again, this is evidence that the conditions at the time and not her age were the cause of her losing her homestead.

Range of Writing

Like independent reading, this domain with its single anchor standard (W.CCR.10) is intended to provide students a chance to write and discuss their writing with others (see table 3.6). Importantly, this standard profiles students' growing ability to write for extended periods of time, both in a single sitting, as well as with writing that develops over the course of time. But it doesn't mean that a student is simply stuck in a corner for forty-five minutes and told to write something while the teacher paces anxiously the whole time. Students need instructional conditions that build toward independence. This includes finding out how other authors compose, especially in their close analysis of reading materials. Students require practice under the guidance of their teacher. Additionally, students need a classroom climate that communicates a belief that writing is an expressive channel that is equally important as speaking. In order for students to meet the writing standard routinely over extended time frames, they must write frequently and fluently to build their stamina for independent writing.

Table 3.6: Writing Standards for Domain Range of Writing, Grades 3–5

Anchor Standard	Grade 3 Standard	Grade 4 Standard	Grade 5 Standard
W.CCR.10: Write routinely and for extended time frames (time for research, reflection, and revision) and shorter time frames (a single sitting or a day or two) for a range of tasks, purposes, and audiences.	**W.3.10:** Write routinely over extended time frames (time for research, reflection, and revision) and shorter time frames (a single sitting or a day or two) for a range of discipline-specific tasks, purposes, and audiences.	**W.4.10:** Write routinely over extended time frames (time for research, reflection, and revision) and shorter time frames (a single sitting or a day or two) for a range of discipline-specific tasks, purposes, and audiences.	**W.5.10:** Write routinely over extended time frames (time for research, reflection, and revision) and shorter time frames (a single sitting or a day or two) for a range of discipline-specific tasks, purposes, and audiences.

Source: Adapted from NGA & CCSSO, 2010a, pp. 18 and 21.

The Writing Process

As with other strands in the Common Core State Standards, writing doesn't isolate one standard while ignoring others within or across strands. Young writers require ongoing multidimensional instruction that fulfills the expectations of the CCSS. Interactive and personal writing experiences enable students to grow in their understanding of what they need to do to write well. Writing behavior is modeled in shared and guided writing activities during which students take turns contributing ideas, dictating words or sentences, or transcribing the message. As students observe writing and participate in the development of a piece, they become aware of appropriate writing behaviors and can begin to apply what they have observed to their personal and independent writing.

- Good writers know effective habits of writing will increase the efficiency and quality of their writing. Young writers need to learn how to organize materials, how to utilize reference materials to support content, and what skills they need to get their ideas down on paper.

- Good writers know how to move from ideas to words to sentences and paragraphs. The less adept writer will be frustrated with his or her inability to transmit ideas to the reader. Writing craft includes word choice and perspective and recognizing that different genres require different approaches.

- Good writers use punctuation, spelling, and grammatical structures to ensure that readers understand their message. Selecting the correct genre of writing to fit the purpose goes hand in hand with the conventions associated with clear writing.

Aspects of the Writing Process

Good writers understand that there is a process to writing and that their awareness of the process can facilitate writing. Writing teacher and researcher Donald Graves (personal communication as cited in Nagin, 2003) writes:

> The writing process is anything a writer does from the time the idea came until the piece is completed or abandoned. There is no particular order. So it's not effective to teach writing process in a lock-step, rigid manner. What a good writing teacher does is help students see where writing comes from; in a chance remark or an article that really burns you up. I still hold by my original statement: if kids don't write more than three days a week they're dead, and it's very hard to become a writer. If you provide frequent occasions for writing then the students start to think about writing when they're not doing it. I call it a constant state of composition. (p. 23)

While we do not advocate for a strictly sequential approach to writing that moves students through a lockstep system, we do believe students will find benefit from learning common writing techniques. Five common writing dimensions are the following.

1. **Prewriting:** Formulating (or brainstorming) ideas that may or may not be utilized later in a writing piece

2. **Drafting:** Committing brainstormed ideas to paper to produce a first draft

3. **Revising:** Revisiting the draft to add, delete, or change what has been drafted

4. **Editing:** Approaching the piece's final form and asking teachers or peers for corrections and feedback on content

5. **Publishing:** Finalizing the piece and sharing it with others

These dimensions build on one another to contribute to the writer's growing stamina and fluency in order to *get in the zone*. If you like sports, you know what it means to be *in the zone*. Athletes in the zone report feeling that time is suspended and that their movements are fluid. Similarly, some people report *getting lost* in a book or good movie. Mihaly Csikszentmihalyi (1997) calls this phenomenon *flow*. He believes that flow is an optimal experience for humans. Fluent writers also gain a sense of flow as they write.

The Characteristics of Flow

In simple terms, Csikszentmihalyi's research suggests that people are generally unhappy doing nothing, happy doing things, and uncertain about what makes them happy. However, people fully engaged in a task *get lost* in the activity or *get in the zone* or what he likes to call *flow*. According to Csikszentmihalyi (1997), there are a number of characteristics of flow, which include the following.

- **Complete involvement, focus, and concentration:** Being innately curious or as the result of having training

- **A sense of ecstasy:** Being outside everyday reality

- **A great inner clarity:** Knowing what needs to be done and how well it is going

- **Knowledge that the activity is doable:** Knowing that one's skills are adequate and that the task does not create anxiety or boredom

- **A sense of serenity:** Not worrying about self; feeling of growing beyond the boundaries of ego—afterward feeling of transcending ego in ways not thought possible

- **Timeliness:** Thoroughly focusing on the present; not noticing time passing

- **Intrinsic motivation:** Using whatever produces flow as a reward

Source: Adapted from Csikszentmihalyi, 1997.

As you can imagine, a goal of teachers is to keep students in flow for as much of the school day as possible. Csikszentmihalyi (1997, 2000) notes humans cannot be in flow all of the time—it is an optimal state, not necessarily a common state of being. When the challenge is relatively high and skills are relatively low, students become anxious. Importantly, when the challenge is relatively low and skills are relatively high, students become bored. When both are low, a profound sense of apathy is apparent.

We believe that flow is influenced in part by fluency in reading and writing. Not being able to read smoothly and accurately is frustrating, causes anxiety, and results in poor comprehension. The message as the brain processes becomes halting, choppy, and disjointed. A similar phenomenon occurs with disfluent writing. When ideas are coming faster that one can write, students become frustrated. If they do not have good command of spelling and vocabulary, they oversimplify their sentences with low-level words and ideas or give up altogether on their writing. Alternatively, smooth and accurate reading allows the reader to concentrate on the meaning of the message, an important contributor to motivation and interest. Likewise, the ability to compose a message without having to stop after every word to recall spelling or syntax allows the writer to concentrate on more sophisticated writing behaviors, such as planning, composing, and revising to create the best message. Without a doubt, fluency in reading and writing is important because they contribute to the learner's ability to fully engage with the literacy activity.

Aspects of Writing Fluency

Writing fluency has received significantly less research attention compared with reading fluency. However, it stands to reason that not writing quickly enough would be frustrating for students. Imagine having all kinds of ideas in your head, but having them leave you before you can record them! Similarly, poor writing volume results in few words to edit. After all, if a student only generates a few dozen words after fifteen minutes of writing, he or she will not have much to edit and revise. Most importantly, a focus on writing fluency requires that students move on with the task and not procrastinate. We've all watched a student staring off into space after being asked to respond in writing to a question or comment. When asked, this student will respond, "I'm thinking" or "I'm not sure what to write." A focus on writing fluency provides students with the skills to record their thoughts, supplies them with ideas to edit and revise, and addresses the frequent delays associated with writing performance. (See pages 92–94 for sample activities to focus on writing fluency.)

While there are a number of theories about writing and how to write, writers generally use three interactive and recursive components: "*planning* what to say, *translating* those plans into written text, and *reviewing* those written texts or plans" (McCutchen, Covill, Hoyne, & Mildes, 1994, p. 256). We maintain that a focus on writing fluency requires attention to each of these three components.

Planning the Message

During planning students must develop the skills to rapidly organize their thinking and develop a scheme for their ideas. Naturally there are a number of strategies that focus on this component, including brainstorming ideas, talking to a partner, thinking and searching through texts, and developing concept maps. A study of fourth- and fifth-grade students reveals those who receive intentional instruction in planning activities produce higher-quality writing than those who receive only process writing instruction in which students revise papers based on teacher feedback (Troia & Graham, 2002).

Translating the Message

As students translate their plans into text, they must have developed the motor skills for extended writing tasks, have the stamina to write for extended periods, and be able to make connections between what they've written and what they're thinking. Predictably, there are specific instructional strategies to help students develop this component, including quick writes, freewrites, timed writings, and power writing. (See pages 92–94 for more information on these instructional strategies.)

Reviewing the Message

In terms of reviewing, students need to be able to read what they've written and revise accordingly. Again, it's important to note that writing is recursive and interactive—writers revise as they write and think as they revise and so on. Once again, intentional instruction in revision has been shown to produce longer and more sophisticated essays. Gary Robert Muschla (1993) suggests that all students be taught a simple five-step plan for revision.

1. Read the piece silently and then aloud. Reading it aloud can highlight the flow and rhythm of the words.

2. Consider the whole piece first. What are its strengths? What parts do you like best? What are its weaknesses? How can the weaknesses be improved? What can be added? What can be eliminated?

3. Focus on the paragraphs. Are they well organized? Does each have a main idea supported by details? Do the paragraphs follow each other logically? Are the transitions between them smooth?

4. Consider the sentences. Do they follow logically? Are they clear?

5. Focus on the words and phrases. Which should be changed? What are examples of clutter? (pp. 62–63)

There is no expected writing fluency rate that can provide teachers guidance with determining how many words per minute students should be able to write. In a study of fourth graders who receive intentional writing instruction in fluency, the class average increased from ten words per minute to twenty-five words per minute (Kasper-Ferguson & Moxley, 2002). The fastest writer in the study began in October writing an average of twenty words per minute and could sustain fifty-nine words per minute in May. Importantly, these researchers note, "Ceiling effects in writing did not appear" (Kasper-Ferguson & Moxley, 2002, p. 249). In other words, students continued to make progress, and given enough time, there was no telling how many words per minute they could have written. At some point, fluency is sufficient and further attempts to increase written production will compromise writing quality. The point is that students need practice getting their ideas on paper such that they have content to edit and revise.

Fluency and Writing Maturity

As with reading, writing fluency is not only about writing more words. As students become more fluent writers, they also become more sophisticated writers. V. Andree Bayliss and Nancy Walker (1990) and Bayliss (1994) identify signs of maturing writing fluency, including:

- Providing details
- Elaborating on the subject
- Varying sentence patterns

- Deepening and unfolding the presentation
- Sustaining focus

As writers become more fluent, they are able to use these devices to produce more sophisticated pieces of writing. When a writer adds detail, the reader can visualize the setting and characters. Elaboration on a subject helps the reader to more fully understand what the writer is discussing (the sentences in this paragraph are examples of elaboration). Additionally, a mature writer can deepen and unfold a presentation by building on concepts in a logical manner. Finally, a good writer does not wander from topic to topic. Taken together, these characteristics form the definition of good writing and an effective writer. Think back to our description of a self-extending writer (page 69). Educators in grades 3–5 play an important role in establishing the foundations students will need to become mature writers.

Writing fluency is important in the elementary classroom because it contributes to more sophisticated expression of ideas. Reading fluency contributes to more sophisticated understanding of ideas. Neither reading nor writing fluency exist in isolation, but rather are influenced by a learner's control of phonics, syntax, comprehension, and vocabulary. However, fluency serves as an important bridge between these processes. Instruction in reading and writing fluency contributes to improving literacy skills of students.

Power Writing

Power writing is a daily instructional routine to build writing fluency. It involves brief, timed writing events. Fearn and Farnan (2001) describe it as "a structured free-write where the objective is quantity alone" (p. 501). Typically, this exercise is performed daily in three rounds of timed writes, each one minute in length. Students are given a word or phrase to use somewhere in their writing and are reminded to "write as much as you can, as well as you can" (Fearn & Farnan, 2001, p. 196). At the end of one minute, they count the number of words they have written and note the total in the margin. This cycle is repeated two more times using different words or phrases. After the last cycle, they re-read what they have written and circle words they believe they may have misspelled. This allows the teacher to evaluate students' self-monitoring of their spelling. They keep a graph where they list the highest number of words for the day.

The purpose of tracking progress is not to establish a competitive atmosphere; these graphs are kept in the writer's notebook, which only the teacher or student views. These simple charts can be constructed on graph paper. See figure 3.5 (page 93) for a sample graph. The words per minute are recorded on the vertical axis and should begin with a number that is just below the writer's current range of words. The teacher establishes this value based on the student's power writing average and his or her goal for each student. For instance, if a writer currently averages thirty-two words per minute, the first square might begin with twenty-five.

Students completing three sessions of power writing are likely to observe another unexpected benefit. Typically, performance increases between the first and third

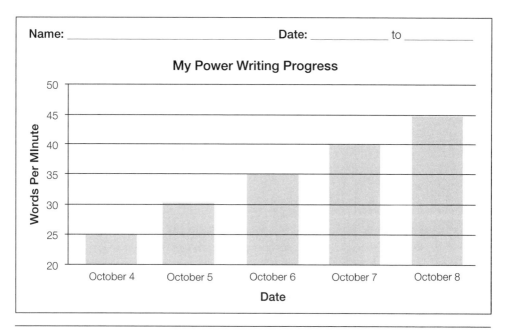

Figure 3.5: Sample power writing graph.

Visit **go.solution-tree.com/commoncore** for a reproducible version of this figure.

rotation. Like physical exercise, the repetitions result in increased fluidity of writing. By assessing their own progress, students internalize their own motivation as they seek to improve on their last effort. This is especially important for struggling writers, who commonly say they "don't know what to write about." If they are stuck, they should be instructed to write the prompt word repeatedly until an idea formulates. As they do so, they begin to think of related words and often start to generate ideas, even if it is only a list of words at the start.

Journal Writing

An effective instructional program provides many opportunities for children to write across subjects and throughout the school day and week. As Graves notes, "If you provide frequent occasions for writing then the students start to think about writing when they're not doing it" (personal communication as cited in Nagin, 2003, p. 23). To help children observe and appreciate their growth as writers, we believe that every student should have a place to keep his or her writing. This is often accomplished through the use of a writing journal. Although organization of the writer's notebook varies by teacher, grade level, and purpose, most are arranged chronologically. Therefore, the various writing exercises during shared, guided, and collaborative writing are likely to be in the notebook or writing folder. We recommend devoting a section of the notebook to fluency exercises like power writing. During independent writing, we sometimes invite students to review past power writing work in the journal and select one to expand into a more finished piece. Students frequently discover a good idea that they had previously overlooked.

The students in Cristina Lopez's third-grade classroom use their writer's notebooks as a tool for conferring with their teacher about their writing progress. She is conducting a writing conference with Artemio about the status of an autobiographical essay he is developing, which began as a power writing piece. She begins by having him read a favorite part.

> "In ten years I could see myself being in 12th grade. I could see myself being a 12th grader because I'm smart, I'm intelegent, and a nice guy. I could also see myself been a driving instructror. I hope I have an excellent life."

Although Artemio has made a few spelling and grammatical errors, Ms. Lopez does not begin with that topic. She makes a few notes about these details, then asks him, "What do you want help with today?" Artemio replies that he had read his essay to another classmate who told him the second paragraph confused her. "I'm not sure how to fix it," he offers. Ms. Lopez replies, "How about if I read it to you, and you can just listen to see what it's missing." She then reads the paragraph while Artemio listens as she reads a paragraph about attending his grandparent's wedding. "Is that what you meant to tell the reader?" she asks.

"Well, I was trying to tell them about when my grandma and grandpa had another wedding because they had been married for like fifty years. We all went to the wedding and it was fun. It seems kind of confusing, though," replies Artemio.

The teacher and student then spend the next few minutes creating a list of details he wants to include about the wedding. "When a writer has to share a series of ideas, they write a list so they don't forget anything," Ms. Lopez replies. When Artemio leaves the conference, he will rewrite this paragraph. Once completed, he will ask Angelica, his peer classmate, to see if the message is clearer.

"I'll see you soon, Artie," says the teacher as she sends him off to his desk. "I can't wait to hear what happened at that wedding!"

Freewriting

Students also need time to write for their own purposes and should be encouraged to write for their own motivation. We return to the concept we discussed earlier—*flow*. Peter Elbow (1981) describes a process called *freewriting* as a method for opening creative pathways. For ten minutes a day, students write independently on a topic of their own choice. During this time, no editing takes place. The sole purpose is to get words down on paper. This differs somewhat from power writing in that it is not viewed as a competition against the clock but rather a way of accessing ideas. When stuck, writers are instructed to write anything—even squiggles—until the words come again. Sometimes the squiggles give the brain a little time to focus and produce. If a student struggles with language, the teacher may need to meet individually with the student to develop some ideas in collaboration that can be used in future writing sessions. Freewriting can be valuable for students to tap into their understanding of the world and themselves.

Conclusion

Learning to write is not a matter of simply brainstorming, drafting, editing, revising, and publishing. It's much messier than that and occasionally (if we are lucky) reaches a state of flow. Our efforts to foster young writers are focused on enabling them to move closer to that *constant state of composition*. In order for students to become writers who are adept at using different text types, and with different purposes and audiences in mind, they must write throughout the day. If they are to produce and distribute their writing across the classroom and the world, they must write frequently. If students are to engage in research in order to build their knowledge and present it to others, they must write across disciplines. Only fifteen minutes of daily instruction (Gilbert & Graham, 2010) is woefully inadequate if students are to attain these expectations. Simply stated, writing needs to be part of the air that is breathed in every classroom.

Writing is a time when students are provided an opportunity to apply the skills they have been learning to create original texts. Students write for a variety of purposes and have a voice in the choice of topics and in making editing decisions. The type of writing a student engages in is influenced by the developmental level of the student and the purpose for writing. Transitional writers in grades 3–5 use multiple sources of information to influence their writing and utilize techniques for writing to improve the message. The CCSS for writing highlight the importance of writing as a communicative channel across disciplines. Like other aspects of these standards, writing should not be confined to the literacy block, but should be incorporated across the learning day.

As with the reading standards, the Common Core State Standards for writing build on content teachers already know. Writing is a major facet of students' schooling, but the question we have to ask ourselves is, are they getting any better at writing? Research evidence from large-scale writing assessments such as the National Assessment of Educational Progress suggests that there is still a lot of work to be done in this area (Salahu-Din, Persky, & Miller, 2008). Overall, the writing that students do in school is not sufficient for them to be successful in college and careers. Rather than assign writing, teachers have to focus on writing *instruction*. This is where the collaborative planning team can help. As we have noted throughout this chapter, collaborative teams can focus their planning conversations around three questions about the writing standards.

1. **Standards:** What is the essence of this standard?

2. **Instruction:** What teacher actions facilitate this standard in practice?

3. **Formative assessment:** What evidence will we accept that students are learning this standard?

By focusing on these questions, teams will develop a scope and sequence of writing curriculum that is connected with the reading students are doing. Teams will also ensure that writing is integrated into the speaking and listening activities students engage in and that language development is occurring so students can write increasingly sophisticated pieces. As we have noted, the Common Core State Standards are interconnected. The writing standards must be taught in the context of all of the other standards so student competence and confidence is routinely raised.

CHAPTER 4

Implementing the Common Core State Standards for Speaking and Listening and for Language

KEY QUESTIONS

- To what extent does your collaborative team understand the Speaking and Listening standards and the Language standards: What is our current level of knowledge about this standard? How can we increase our expertise? How will we measure our growth?

- How much classroom speaking do students do that is academic in nature? Do they use argumentation and provide evidence for their claims when they share their thinking?

- How sophisticated is the language students use in speaking and writing? Are there language structures that students need to learn to be successful?

Fifth graders Jacob, Sujit, Theresa, Miguel, and Tanja have just begun a new book in their literature circle: *Bud, Not Buddy* (Curtis, 1999). During their last meeting, they agreed to read chapters one and two and assigned literature circle roles. Miguel agrees to be the Vocabulary Enricher for this meeting (Daniels, 2002).

Miguel opens the discussion by stating, "I don't know about the rest of you, but some of the words in the first two chapters were hard. Well, not hard like I had never heard them before, but hard because I didn't know what they were talking about. Did anyone else have that trouble?"

The others nod in agreement, and Miguel continues. "Like right on page two, the woman says, 'I know you don't understand what it means, but there's a depression going on all over this country.' I wasn't sure what depression was."

Tanja, the History Connector, looks excited. "I found it in our social studies book, all about the Great Depression. It was in the 1930s, and lots of people in the United States were poor."

"That makes sense, because look at the next sentence—'People can't find jobs and these are very, very difficult times for everyone'" (Curtis, 1999, p. 2).

At this point, teacher Yvonne Pearman, who had stopped by the group to observe, offers to clarify. She goes on to explain the Great Depression and the lives many people led during this period. "You'll see a lot of vocabulary in this book that sounds old-fashioned because the story is set in the 1930s. This will be a good feature for the Vocabulary Enricher to pay attention to in this book."

Miguel brightens at this. "I found a whole bunch of words that I didn't know how to define. Like *doggone* and *shucks*. No one talks like that anymore."

Ms. Pearman responds, "Exactly, Miguel. Some of the words the author uses are kind of strange to us, and we have to use context clues to figure out what they mean because they're really not dictionary words. As the Vocabulary Enricher, you'll have to decide what words are important and what are just interesting. *The Great Depression* is really important in this book, and it's a concept word. *Doggone* isn't—it's a label word. Good readers pay attention to the words they need to investigate and recognize the words they don't need to spend too much time with."

Theresa, who has been listening quietly to the exchange, joins the conversation. "The Great Depression was during the 1930s, right?" There is a long silence as the others consider this. A little sheepishly, she adds, "Um, when were you born?"

A Collaborative Planning Team in Action

It should come as no surprise that the unit of instruction Ms. Pearman developed for *Bud, Not Buddy* began with her collaborative team's conversations about the Common Core State Standards for English language arts.

"It really began with looking at text complexity," she begins. "We originally taught using this book at the end of fourth grade, but decided to move it to early fifth." Her collaborative team was surprised to learn that the book scored quantitatively higher than they expected—950L. However, it was the team's qualitative assessment that drove the decision to use the book early in fifth grade.

"The Language standard on comparing the use of dialects made this an ideal text to use," Ms. Pearman notes. "Many of the characters use a vernacular that pinpoints a place in time and a region."

The third- through fifth-grade teams also decide they wanted to strengthen their students' ability to discuss texts. Third-grade teachers focus on partner reading, while fourth and fifth grades use reciprocal teaching with informational texts and literature circles with narrative.

"We also decided that we would systematically reduce the external supports over time while increasing the groups' collective responsibility to one another. We're only going to use formal role sheets for this first book study," she says. "We were hanging on to them for way too long and it ended up stymying their discussions. We want them to understand that as participants they need to do, and listen for, all of these aspects, not just the one they were assigned to." She cites the Speaking and Listening standards on comprehension and collaboration as an impetus for this move.

Ms. Pearman's collaborative team approaches its study of the Common Core Speaking and Listening standards, as well as the Language standards, somewhat differently than the Reading and Writing standards.

"We quickly realized that while we knew a lot about reading and writing instruction, we were a bit more in the weeds when it came to these standards and expectations. At first, we weren't even in agreement about what language is," she says. "We really needed to keep going back to three guiding questions," Ms. Pearman says.

1. What is our current level of knowledge about this standard?

2. How can we increase our expertise?

3. How will we measure our growth?

"We needed to be able to build our own knowledge before we could ever hope to build our students,'" she says.

Figure 4.1 (pages 100–101) and figure 4.2 (page 102) offer sample protocols you can use in your collaborative team to analyze the Language standards and Speaking and Listening standards, using the three guiding questions from Ms. Pearman and her collaborative team. (Visit **go.solution-tree.com/commoncore** for online-only reproducibles of these figures.)

Because the Speaking and Listening strand and the Language strand are interrelated, we will examine them together in this chapter. Language is not only confined to oral and verbal ability; it supports it. Like Ms. Pearman's collaborative planning team, we hope this lens is useful in reducing the temptation to isolate the Common Core State Standards to the extent that they lose their usefulness. In other words, when planning lessons, collaborative teams should not focus only on one strand, be that Reading, Writing, Speaking and Listening, or Language. Instead, they should identify opportunities to address appropriate standards from each area.

Anchor Standards for Speaking and Listening

The anchor standards for Speaking and Listening spotlight the quality of transactions students have across the table, classroom, and world. NGA and CCSSO (2010a) note, "Students must have ample opportunities to take part in a variety of rich, structured conversations—as part of a whole class, in small groups, and with a partner" (p. 22). In the 21st century, in which digital communications have become a feature of everyday life, these communication skills extend to virtual environments. These anchor standards are divided into two domains: (1) Comprehension and Collaboration and (2) Presentation of Knowledge and Ideas. Together, they outline the expectations for the informal and formal talk of an effective classroom. As you and your collaborative team examine these standards, notice how they clearly link to those discussed in the Reading and Writing strands in chapters 2 and 3.

Language anchor standard three (L.CCR.3): Apply knowledge of language to understand how language functions in different contexts, to make effective choices for meaning or style, and to comprehend when reading or listening.

CCSS grade band: Grades 3–5

Anchor standard domain: Knowledge of Language

Grade-Level Standard	What Is Our Current Level of Knowledge About This Standard?	How Can We Increase Our Expertise?	How Will We Measure Our Growth?
Grade 3			
L.3.3: Use knowledge of language and its conventions when writing, speaking, reading, or listening. a. Choose words and phrases for effect.* b. Recognize and observe differences between the conventions of spoken and written standard English.			
Grade 4			
L.4.3: Use knowledge of language and its conventions when writing, speaking, reading, or listening. a. Choose words and phrases to convey ideas precisely.* b. Choose punctuation for effect.* c. Differentiate between contexts that call for formal English (such as when presenting ideas) and situations in which informal discourse is appropriate (like in small-group discussion).			

Grade-Level Standard	What Is Our Current Level of Knowledge About This Standard?	How Can We Increase Our Expertise?	How Will We Measure Our Growth?
Grade 5 **L.5.3:** Use knowledge of language and its conventions when writing, speaking, reading, or listening. a. Expand, combine, and reduce sentences for meaning, reader and listener interest, and style. b. Compare and contrast the varieties of English (such as in dialects and registers) used in stories, dramas, or poems.			

* These standards require continued attention in higher grades as they are applied to increasingly sophisticated writing and speaking.

Source: Adapted from NGA & CCSSO, 2010a, p. 29.

Figure 4.1: Guiding questions for grade-by-grade analysis of the Language standards.

Visit **go.solution-tree.com/commoncore** for a reproducible version of this figure.

Speaking and Listening anchor standard five (SL.CCR.5): Make strategic use of digital media and visual displays of data to express information and enhance understanding of presentations.

CCSS grade band: Grades 3–5

Anchor standard domain: Knowledge of Language

Grade-Level Standards	What Is Our Current Level of Knowledge About This Standard?	How Can We Increase Our Expertise?	How Will We Measure Our Growth?
Grade 3 **SL.3.5:** Create engaging audio recordings of stories or poems that demonstrate fluid reading at an understandable pace; add visual displays when appropriate to emphasize or enhance certain facts or details.			
Grade 4 **SL.4.5:** Add audio recordings and visual displays to presentations when appropriate to enhance the development of main ideas or themes.			
Grade 5 **SL.5.5:** Include multimedia components (like graphics and sound) and visual displays in presentations when appropriate to enhance the development of main ideas or themes.			

Source: Adapted from NGA & CCSSO, 2010a, p. 24.

Figure 4.2: Guiding questions for grade-by-grade analysis of the Speaking and Listening standards.

Visit go.solution-tree.com/commoncore for a reproducible version of this figure.

Comprehension and Collaboration

The three anchor standards in this domain focus on the student's growing ability to collaborate with others in a meaningful way, using the content as the platform for their work. Anchor standard one (SL.CCR.1) describes the dispositions of the prepared student who can fully participate in academic discussions. Anchor standard three (SL.CCR.3) is reminiscent of the work on accountable talk, which describes the habits of speakers and listeners as they engage in academic discourse, such as incorporating the statements of others into the discussion, asking questioning, using evidence and examples, and even disagreeing with one another (Michaels, O'Connor, & Resnick, 2008). Anchor standard two (SL.CCR.2) bridges the other two standards, as it reminds us of the role that content knowledge plays in these conversations.

1. Prepare for and participate effectively in a range of conversations and collaborations with diverse partners, building on others' ideas and expressing their own clearly and persuasively. (SL.CCR.1)

2. Integrate and evaluate information presented in diverse media and formats, including visually, quantitatively, and orally. (SL.CCR.2)

3. Evaluate a speaker's point of view, reasoning, and use of evidence and rhetoric. (SL.CCR.3) (NGA & CCSSO, 2010a, p. 22)

Presentation of Knowledge and Ideas

The second domain of anchor standards for the Speaking and Listening strand profiles the essential nature of presenting information to one another in more formal ways. Anchor standard four (SL.CCR.4) discusses the ways a speaker organizes and presents information, always keeping the audience and the purpose for the presentation in mind. Anchor standard six (SL.CCR.6) is a reminder that presenters are also listeners and consumers of information. As such, they need to use critical-thinking skills in order to make judgments about the information being shared. Anchor standard five (SL.CCR.5) serves to bridge these two ideas, and it focuses on the presenter's skills in using digital media and visual displays of information, as well as the listener's ability to understand it.

4. Present information, findings, and supporting evidence such that listeners can follow the line of reasoning and the organization, development, and style are appropriate to task, purpose, and audience. (SL.CCR.4)

5. Make strategic use of digital media and visual displays of data to express information and enhance understanding of presentations. (SL.CCR.5)

6. Adapt speech to a variety of contexts and communicative tasks, demonstrating command of formal English when indicated or appropriate. (SL.CCR.6) (NGA & CCSSO, 2010a, p. 22)

Taken together, the anchor standards for Speaking and Listening highlight the integral role of peers in the learning process. Long gone is the notion that all knowledge emanates from the teacher and that the student's chief role is to listen quietly and take it all in (Frey et al., 2009). Peer learning has become a dominant feature in 21st century classrooms, which carries implications for tomorrow's citizens. These standards are not about being able to pass on pleasantries to one another; they are the engine of learning. Before we examine the specific Speaking and Listening standards for grades 3–5, we consider what is known about peer learning.

The Power of Peer Learning

Perhaps the most influential theorist on the role of peer-assisted learning is Lev Vygotsky (1978), who states that all learning is the product of sociocultural phenomena mediated by interactions with others. These social interactions shape the learner's view of the world. Therefore, collaboration with peers becomes a necessary part of a child's learning process. Indeed, Vygotsky identifies both the teacher and peers as important agents in the learning process (Crain, 2000).

One of Vygotsky's (1978) most enduring contributions to education is the concept of a *zone of proximal development*, which describes tasks a learner can successfully complete with minimal assistance. Students who assist one another in completing a task that might otherwise be too difficult for either to complete alone are considered to be working within their zone of proximal development. Many of us have found ourselves working in a group in which the problem is solved through discussion. This is why collaborative planning teams are so powerful; we all enjoy learning and producing in the presence of our peers. So it is with peer learning.

In addition to solving the task at hand, another goal of this type of learning is to foster mastery of skills and strategies that can be used independently in the future. This learning occurs when these "external and social activities are gradually internalized by the child . . . creat[ing] internal dialogues that form the processes of mental regulation" (Wood, 1998, p. 98). Stated differently, the language two students use to figure out a task together eventually becomes part of the internal problem-solving processes each child uses independently.

The power of peer-to-peer learning has been well documented in the research base on effective instruction, and it lies at the heart of all academic discussions (Mueller & Fleming, 2001; Stevens & Slavin, 1995). When students work collaboratively on a task, they are able to clarify one another's understandings, explore possible solutions, analyze concepts, and create new products (Frey et al., 2009). Additionally, they provide an ideal arena for the teacher to observe learning as it takes place, especially through listening to the problem-solving strategies that students use as they wrestle with concepts, skills, and ideas. The anchor standards articulate a path for students to regularly engage in these kinds of collaborative learning processes so that students can construct—not just assimilate—knowledge and share it with others. In the next section, we will examine how peer learning forms the basis for the Speaking and Listening standards for grades 3–5.

Speaking and Listening Standards for Grades 3–5

The six grade-level standards for Speaking and Listening are organized in the same manner as the domains they are derived from: Comprehension and Collaboration and Presentation of Knowledge and Ideas. Using the protocol in figures 4.1 and 4.2, consider the following questions in your collaborative team:

- What is our current level of knowledge about this standard?

- How can we increase our expertise?

- How will we measure our growth?

Alternatively, you and your team may prefer to use the analysis questions from chapters 2 and 3 (pages 29 and 62). Whichever set of questions you select to guide your discussions, you will be working within a framework that enables you to better understand and implement the CCSS.

Comprehension and Collaboration

The three standards in this domain describe the dispositions and purposes of informal talk in the classroom (see table 4.1, page 106). Throughout grades 3–5, students are expected to be prepared to participate in discussions with peers, especially as it applies to prerequisite work. For example, if any of the students in Ms. Pearman's literature circle had failed to read the first chapter in advance of their discussion, the quality of the talk would have suffered. Instead, it was elevated because they were able to cite examples in the text as evidence of their comments and questions.

Another notable feature of this domain is that its standards are intertwined with other domains of the Common Core ELA standards. For example, collaborative reading experiences provide students with opportunities to make meaning of a text with their peers. When students read and discuss together, they apply comprehension strategies and support the understanding of others. We use *collaborative reading* as an umbrella term to describe a number of peer-reading activities, including partner reading, collaborative strategic reading, literature circles, and reciprocal teaching. While each of these peer-reading arrangements possesses unique features, there are common elements.

First, students work in pairs or groups of no more than five. Second, the work they do is outside the immediate supervision of the teacher. Instead, they guide their own discussions and make decisions about how the task will be completed. A third element common to these collaborative reading practices is that students work with text to deepen their understanding of the content and the processes they use to comprehend. The Comprehension and Collaboration standards should be viewed through the lens of the content being taught, not held in isolation of other literacy and discipline-specific expectations.

Table 4.1: Speaking and Listening Standards for Domain Comprehension and Collaboration, Grades 3–5

Anchor Standard	Grade 3 Standards	Grade 4 Standards	Grade 5 Standards
SL.CCR.1: Prepare for and participate effectively in a range of conversations and collaborations with diverse partners, building on others' ideas and expressing their own clearly and persuasively.	**SL.3.1:** Engage effectively in a range of collaborative discussions (one-on-one, in groups, and teacher-led) with diverse partners on grade 3 topics and texts, building on others' ideas and expressing their own clearly. a. Come to discussions prepared, having read or studied required material; explicitly draw on that preparation and other information known about the topic to explore ideas under discussion. b. Follow agreed-on rules for discussions (such as gaining the floor in respectful ways, listening to others with care, and speaking one at a time about the topics and texts under discussion). c. Ask questions to check understanding of information presented, stay on topic, and link their comments to the remarks of others. d. Explain their own ideas and understanding in light of the discussion.	**SL.4.1:** Engage effectively in a range of collaborative discussions (one-on-one, in groups, and teacher-led) with diverse partners on grade 4 topics and texts, building on others' ideas and expressing their own clearly. a. Come to discussions prepared, having read or studied required material; explicitly draw on that preparation and other information known about the topic to explore ideas under discussion. b. Follow agreed-on rules for discussions and carry out assigned roles. c. Pose and respond to specific questions to clarify or follow up on information, and make comments that contribute to the discussion and link to the remarks of others. d. Review the key ideas expressed and explain their own ideas and understanding in light of the discussion.	**SL.5.1:** Engage effectively in a range of collaborative discussions (one-on-one, in groups, and teacher-led) with diverse partners on grade 5 topics and texts, building on others' ideas and expressing their own clearly. a. Come to discussions prepared, having read or studied required material; explicitly draw on that preparation and other information known about the topic to explore ideas under discussion. b. Follow agreed-on rules for discussions and carry out assigned roles. c. Pose and respond to specific questions by making comments that contribute to the discussion and elaborate on the remarks of others. d. Review the key ideas expressed and draw conclusions in light of information and knowledge gained from the discussions.

SL.CCR.2: Integrate and evaluate information presented in diverse media and formats, including visually, quantitatively, and orally.	**SL.3.2:** Determine the main ideas and supporting details of a text read aloud or information presented in diverse media and formats, including visually, quantitatively, and orally.	**SL.4.2:** Paraphrase portions of a text read aloud or information presented in diverse media and formats, including visually, quantitatively, and orally.	**SL.5.2:** Summarize a written text read aloud or information presented in diverse media and formats, including visually, quantitatively, and orally.
SL.CCR.3: Evaluate a speaker's point of view, reasoning, and use of evidence and rhetoric.	**SL.3.3:** Ask and answer questions about information from a speaker, offering appropriate elaboration and detail.	**SL.4.3:** Identify the reasons and evidence a speaker provides to support particular points.	**SL.5.3:** Summarize the points a speaker makes and explain how each claim is supported by reasons and evidence.

Source: Adapted from NGA & CCSSO, 2010a, pp. 22 and 24.

Grade 3 standard one (SL.3.1c) specifically calls out questioning to check for understanding as an expectation for small-group and whole-class discussions. It can be difficult for young students to examine the quality of their questions because they quickly forget their questions and think of new ones.

Art Matsumoto, a third-grade teacher, is helping his students develop an interview protocol for a class project on family biographies. He reads aloud family narratives like *Little House on the Prairie* (Wilder, 2010) and excerpts of *Cheaper by the Dozen* (Gilbreth & Carey, 2002) to profile the importance of anecdotes and stories in a family's history. Students construct family trees and a family timeline. Their next assignment is to interview one adult family member to create a biographical essay. Mr. Matsumoto knows that his students will need to structure the interview if they are to assemble useful notes.

"I want them to see that preparing questions in advance is helpful when planning for an interview. And I want them to realize that the quality of their questions when we're working together can really affect the outcome of their task," he says.

Mr. Matsumoto introduces the lesson by explaining that an interview protocol is a method writers use to remember to ask important questions and take good notes. "A good idea for taking notes is to leave spaces between the questions so that when they give you an answer, you can write it down easily," he says. Mr. Matsumoto then tells the class that he is going to interview Ms. Jefferson, the teacher next door, while they watch. He then shows them the interview protocol he previously constructed on chart paper. It contains three questions.

1. How old are you?

2. What is your favorite thing about teaching third grade?

3. Do you remember when you first met me?

Ms. Jefferson arrives and takes a seat in front of the class. He begins by asking her how old she is, and she tells him politely that it is none of his business. Mr. Matsumoto writes this down and asks the second question about teaching third grade. She replies that eight-year-olds ask interesting questions that make her think about the world in new ways. Again, Mr. Matsumoto writes this down on the chart paper while the students watch. He then asks her his final question, and she gives a one-word response: "Yes." Again, he scribes her answer and thanks her for her time.

Having created a shared experience, he is now ready to turn the discussion over to them. "I have two things I'd like for you to think about. Do these questions give me the information I want? How can I improve them?"

What ensues is a lively discussion about the appropriateness of the first question. Jordan volunteers, "My dad told me it's not nice to ask ladies how old they are." Mr. Matsumoto then remarks that some men as well as women don't like to answer that question.

The class agrees that the second question is a good one and thinks that it should be kept because Ms. Jefferson's answer was interesting. They also agree that the third question is a problem because he only got a one-word answer from Ms. Jefferson. Linnette suggests changing the question to read, "What do you remember about the first time we met?" and Mr. Matsumoto adds that to the list.

He then invites them to suggest other questions for use in an interview protocol. After scribing five of them, he instructs the students to work in partners to develop two more questions. While the pairs work together, he checks for understanding. Several minutes later, he signals an end to the partner work and writes down the students' suggestions on the growing list. When he's finished, he tells the class, "Now we've got a long list of possible questions. You don't want to use them all, and some of them won't work in your interview. What I'd like you to do during activity time is select eight to ten questions for your interview protocol. You can rewrite and reword them in any way." With that, these third graders get to work on developing an interview instrument for their biographical essay.

Both anchor standard one (SL.CCR.1) and anchor standard two (SL.CCR.2) in this domain acknowledge the vital role of gaining information from other sources. In the first standard, the attention is on how we do so in conversations and discussions with others. In the second standard, the focus is on how we also acquire information from other speakers who use informational displays and other forms of multimedia technology to share their information. Standard two reflects the increasing importance of visual literacy and informational graphics for displaying and comprehending information (Frey & Fisher, 2008). The 21st century textbooks are filled with more photographs, charts, and diagrams than ever before. Even the ancillary materials rely on multimedia presentations. Short video clips are designed to build background knowledge at the beginning of a unit. Interviews with experts on the topic being studied are offered as a means to supplement print resources. Increasingly, these print resources are being converted to digital texts. However, these digital formats can tax the listening-comprehension skills of students.

Fourth-grade social studies teacher Mae Saunders uses oral history recordings from her state's historical society to bring voices from the past to life.

"These are great resources, but I realized that my students didn't know *how* to listen to these," Ms. Saunders says. "Some of the recordings are old and scratchy, and the audio quality isn't what they're accustomed to. But what was even more difficult was that they didn't know what to listen for."

Since these were recordings of people describing their personal memory of an event, such as a person who attended Martin Luther King Jr.'s "I Have a Dream" speech in 1963, she taught her students to listen to it as a form of journalism. "I tell them we have to think of ourselves as reporters, and listen for the who, what, when, where, why, and how of the story the person is telling." Ms. Saunders says that this helps her students to listen closely and make notes.

"The students set up their notebook page with the who, what, when, where, why, and how question stems and leave a few lines of space between each. As the person on the audio recording tells his or her story, the students write down the details. When it's finished, we've got a basis for our discussion."

Activities like the one Ms. Saunders uses hold the additional benefit of addressing standard three's focus on gathering and summarizing the speaker's information. You may recall third-grade teacher Ms. Hutchinson's explanation in chapter 3 (page 79) of how she uses VoiceThread (www.voicethread.com), a digital storyboard website. Her students create multimedia presentations and record their voices to accompany the still images they have designed. Classmates listen to and respond to the digital storyboards and are able to leave their comments and questions as a permanent part of the presentation.

"I like that there's a record of the conversation in a virtual environment, because it allows them, and me, to capture discussion in a more permanent way," Ms. Hutchinson says. Ms. Hutchison requires each viewer to ask at least two questions for the speaker, and in turn each speaker needs to return to the presentation to answer them. "Last year when I was taking a graduate course at the local university, I had a number of online discussion boards that I had to participate in," she recalls. "It occurred to me that my third graders are doing something very similar!"

Presentation of Knowledge and Ideas

Anchor standards four through six (SL.CCR.4, 5, and 6) of this domain mirror those in the preceding domain. While the first three standards emphasize informal talk, these address the formal talk of presentations. As well, they describe the necessary skills the speaker should exhibit (see table 4.2). Efficient presentation skills, whether face-to-face or in a digital environment, requires the speaker to follow these constructs:

- Organize the information into a logical sequence so that listeners and viewers can comprehend it

- Have a deep and accurate subject knowledge of the topic

- Ensure graphically displayed information is coherent, accurate, well designed, grammatically correct, and free of misspellings

- Deliver the information smoothly and give attention to the audience's needs (for example, eye contact, elocution, and so on)

Grades 3–5 students are not experienced in the demands of formal presentations and are likely to need considerable support in sharing their knowledge with others in formal ways. It's helpful to tie these formal presentations to the writing standards, as presentations are usually written before they are delivered. Given that there is a parallel emphasis on organization in the writing standards, students should be encouraged to convert these written products into formal presentations. The *paragraph frame* is a useful instructional scaffold for doing both. It is a series of sentence stems intended to scaffold original writing while furnishing an organizational structure. Paragraph frames are not intended as fill-in-the-blank exercises. Instead, they should be introduced after rich oral development of ideas and concepts. This preliminary stage of oral composition assists

Table 4.2: Speaking and Listening Standards for Domain Presentation of Knowledge and Ideas, Grades 3–5

Anchor Standards	Grade 3 Standards	Grade 4 Standards	Grade 5 Standards
SL.CCR.4: Present information, findings, and supporting evidence such that listeners can follow the line of reasoning and the organization, development, and style are appropriate to task, purpose, and audience.	**SL.3.4:** Report on a topic or text, tell a story, or recount an experience with appropriate facts and relevant, descriptive details, speaking clearly at an understandable pace.	**SL.4.4:** Report on a topic or text, tell a story, or recount an experience in an organized manner, using appropriate facts and relevant, descriptive details to support main ideas or themes; speak clearly at an understandable pace.	**SL.5.4:** Report on a topic or text or present an opinion, sequencing ideas logically and using appropriate facts and relevant, descriptive details to support main ideas or themes; speak clearly at an understandable pace.
SL.CCR.5: Make strategic use of digital media and visual displays of data to express information and enhance understanding of the presentations.	**SL.3.5:** Create engaging audio recordings of stories or poems that demonstrate fluid reading at an understandable pace; add visual displays when appropriate to emphasize or enhance certain facts or details.	**SL.4.5:** Add audio recordings and visual displays to presentations when appropriate to enhance the development of main ideas or themes.	**SL.5.5:** Include multimedia components (like graphics and sound) and visual displays in presentations when appropriate to enhance the development of main ideas or themes.
SL.CCR.6: Adapt speech to a variety of contexts and communicative tasks, demonstrating command of formal English when indicated or appropriate.	**SL.3.6:** Speak in complete sentences when appropriate to task and situation in order to provide requested detail or clarification. (See grade 3 Language standards one and three on for specific expectations.)	**SL.4.6:** Differentiate between contexts that call for formal English (such as when presenting ideas) and situations where informal discourse is appropriate (like in small-group discussion); use formal English when appropriate to task and situation. (See grade 4 Language standard one for specific expectations.)	**SL.5.6:** Adapt speech to a variety of contexts and tasks, using formal English when appropriate to task and situation. (See grade 5 Language standards one and three for specific expectations.)

Source: Adapted from NGA & CCSSO, 2010a, pp. 22 and 24.

writers in organizing their own thoughts about a topic as they engage in informal talk (see standards one to three in table 4.1, page 106). The paragraph frame is introduced, and students are instructed to add original sentences within or after it. This procedure is more sophisticated than traditional story starters, which begin with a sentence stem, like "It was a dark and stormy night," because it provides more structure for the writer. A paragraph frame might look like this:

"_____ is an important part of my life. When I think about _____ _____. I like to share _____. I could teach you _____."

Notice that the frame establishes a direction for the writer without being prescriptive. Furthermore, the writers do not need to use these sentences in sequence, but can add their own original writing within the frame. As noted previously, writers can also add to or extend the topic further. These frames can be easily created to reflect informational writing as well. For example:

"Hurricanes are violent storms that form over the warm water of the world's oceans. Characteristics of hurricanes are _____. These storms are measured through _____. Warning systems _____. The primary dangers of hurricanes are _____."

Once written, these paragraph frames organize formal presentations as well, especially in sequencing facts, events, or concepts in a logical order. Other sample paragraph frames appear in figure 4.3.

Narrative
They came for me! I wasn't doing anything and then _____. They said, "_____," but I _____. And then _____.
Biographical and Autobiographical
I was thinking about my life. When I was young, _____. But today, _____. The best thing about my life is _____. I am lucky because _____.
Informational and Explanatory
Memorial Day is more than a day off. Memorial Day gave me time to think about _____. I also remembered _____. I know that _____. I miss _____. But _____. I wonder what other people thought about on Memorial Day. I think _____.

Figure 4.3: Sample paragraph frames for writing and formal presentations.

Anchor standard six (SL.CCR.6) for Speaking and Listening specifically references Language standard one on using the conventions of English in speech and in writing. In terms of the speaking portion of the standard, this means using the correct grammar and syntax of conventional English. This can be challenging for students learning English or for some students with language disabilities that make learning English difficult. These students might require more support.

Fourth-grade teacher Jillian Brown uses a simple technique for supporting her students who require additional language support. "We do lots of group presentations in our class, because the collaboration is so valuable," she begins. "But it can be difficult for some students. We do what I like to call *human captioning* to draw on a little more support." As groups organize their presentations into key ideas, they create sentence strips to match. These strips are written in complete sentences, and as a speaker discusses his or her portion of the speech, he or she holds the sentence strip under him. "Like when you watch a news program and there's that text on the bottom of the screen that gives the viewer the main idea of the topic," Ms. Brown explains. This has added benefit for the speaker, as the back of the sentence strip is the place where he or she can write notes. "It keeps the speaker organized to state his ideas correctly, and it helps organize the listeners, too."

Anchor Standards for Language

A final set of Common Core ELA standards is dedicated to language. Speech and language are closely related, but they do have distinct features that make them unique. Speech concerns verbal expression; language describes what words mean (vocabulary), how they are strung together to make sense using the rules of the language (grammar and syntax), how new words are made (conjugation), and what word combinations work best for a situation (pragmatics and register) (American Speech-Language-Hearing Association, 2012). Language is foundational to what we do, and we are so enmeshed in it that it can be difficult to distance ourselves in order to observe it. As the saying goes, "The last thing a fish notices is the water it swims in." Language is to humans as water is to fish. By the way, your ability to understand that last idiom and its analogy speaks to your command of language. The NGA and CCSSO (2010a) put it a different way:

> The inclusion of Language standards in their own strand should not be taken as an indication that skills related to conventions, effective language use, and vocabulary are unimportant to reading, writing, speaking, and listening; indeed, they are inseparable from such contexts. (p. 25)

The overall intent of the Language standards speaks to the need to raise our students' awareness of language, something they are not likely to be able to do without an aware teacher's intentional instruction. As a reminder, you may want to analyze the standards for the grades 3–5 band with these questions in mind: (1) What is our current level of knowledge about this standard? (2) How can we increase our expertise? and (3) How will we measure our growth? In the next section, we will examine the anchor standards for Language, which are foundational to the grade-level standards. They are organized into three dimensions: (1) Conventions of Standard English, (2) Knowledge of Language, and (3) Vocabulary Acquisition and Use.

Conventions of Standard English

This first domain of standards concerns itself with the grammatical rules of spoken and written language, especially as they pertain to parts of speech, written conventions, and spelling. These are essential to communication and involve issues related to the development of complex sentences, as well as voice and mood.

1. Demonstrate command of the conventions of standard English grammar and usage when writing or speaking. (L.CCR.1)

2. Demonstrate command of the conventions of standard English capitalization, punctuation, and spelling when writing. (L.CCR.2) (NGA & CCSSO, 2010a, p. 25)

A unique feature of the CCSS is a table that provides a graphic representation of the language progression for Language standards one to three (see table 4.3). We have reproduced the entire table here; but in grades 3–5, only the first two anchor standards are included. The CCSS expect attention to language demands to continue throughout the grades as they are applied to increasingly sophisticated writing and speaking situations. The table highlights particular skills that are likely to need many years of attention to refine and expand. For example, while subject-verb agreement and pronoun-antecedent agreement is formally introduced in third grade, they should receive attention through twelfth grade.

Knowledge of Language

This domain has a single anchor standard that covers quite a bit of territory. Beginning in grade 2 (there isn't a grade-level standard for this domain in kindergarten or first grade), students begin to attend to the registers of language, especially in comparing formal and informal modes. By high school, students are applying their knowledge of language through the use of style guides, like Modern Language Association (MLA) style. This anchor standard is strongly linked to those in Writing and in Speaking and Listening.

3. Apply knowledge of language to understand how language functions in different contexts, to make effective choices for meaning or style, and to comprehend more fully when reading or listening. (L.CCR.3) (NGA & CCSSO, 2010a, p. 25)

Vocabulary Acquisition and Use

This domain has received considerable attention in the educational community because of the emphasis in anchor standard four (L.CCR.4) on word solving. While this approach to vocabulary development has been widely researched (for example, Baumann, Font, Edwards, & Boland, 2005; Blachowitz & Fisher, 2002), in practice there has been a more prominent focus on vocabulary lists. As anchor standard six (L.CCR.6) illustrates, grade-level vocabulary lists are valuable. Every teacher should have a strong sense of the grade-level vocabulary expectations. However, this should be coupled with purposeful instruction on how to solve for unknown words.

A second area of attention has been on nuanced use of language in standard six. Note that it defines vocabulary as "words and phrases," not single words alone. In addition, it describes these words and phrases as *general academic* and *domain specific*. These terms align with the work of Beck et al. (2002) and their description of tier two words (in the

Table 4.3: Language Progressive Skills by Grade

Standards	Grades							
	3	4	5	6	7	8	9–10	11–12
L.3.1f: Ensure subject-verb and pronoun-antecedent agreement.								
L.3.3a: Choose words and phrases for effect.								
L.4.1f: Produce complete sentences, recognizing and correcting inappropriate fragments and run-ons.								
L.4.1g: Correctly use frequently confused words (such as to/too/two and there/their).[1]								
L.4.3a: Choose words and phrases to convey ideas precisely.[1]								
L.4.3b: Choose punctuation for effect.								
L.5.1d: Recognize and correct inappropriate shifts in verb tense.								
L.5.2a: Use punctuation to separate items in a series.[2]								
L.6.1c: Recognize and correct inappropriate shifts in pronoun number and person.								
L.6.1d: Recognize and correct vague pronouns (such as ones with unclear or ambiguous antecedents).								
L.6.1e: Recognize variations from standard English in their own and others' writing and speaking, and identify and use strategies to improve expression in conventional language.								
L.6.2a: Use punctuation (like commas, parentheses, and dashes) to set off nonrestrictive and parenthetical elements.								
L.6.3a: Vary sentence patterns for meaning, reader and listener interest, and style.[3]								

continued →

Standards	Grades							
	3	4	5	6	7	8	9–10	11–12
L.6.3b: Maintain consistency in style and tone.								
L.7.1c: Place phrases and clauses within a sentence, recognizing and correcting misplaced and dangling modifiers.								
L.7.3a: Choose language that expresses ideas precisely and concisely, recognizing and eliminating wordiness and redundancy.								
L.8.1d: Recognize and correct inappropriate shifts in verb voice and mood.								
L.9–10.1a: Use parallel structure.								

[1] Subsumed by L.7.3a
[2] Subsumed by L.9–10.1a
[3] Subsumed by L.11–12.3a
* The Language standards one to three, are particularly likely to require continued attention in higher grades as they are applied to increasingly sophisticated writing and speaking.

Source: Adapted from NGA & CCSSO, 2010a, p. 30. Used with permission.

language of CCSS, they are general academic words and phrases like *motionless* and *endearing qualities*) that mature language users use in several contexts. In addition, tier three words are those domain-specific words and phrases that are tied to a discipline, like using *nebula* and *recessive genes* in science. Anchor standard five (L.CCR.5) draws attention to the need to appreciate the artistry of words that convey just the right meaning, tone, and mood.

4. Determine or clarify the meaning of unknown and multiple-meaning words and phrases by using context clues, analyzing meaningful word parts, and consulting general and specialized reference materials, as appropriate. (L.CCR.4)

5. Demonstrate understanding of figurative language, word relationships, and nuances in word meanings. (L.CCR.5)

6. Acquire and use accurately a range of general academic and domain-specific words and phrases sufficient for reading, writing, speaking, and listening at the college and career readiness level; demonstrate independence in gathering vocabulary knowledge when encountering an unknown term important to comprehension or expression. (L.CCR.6) (NGA & CCSSO, 2010a, p. 25)

Language Standards for Grades 3–5

The anchor standards frame a pathway for language development from kindergarten through twelfth grade, with an eye toward systematically preparing students for the language demands of career and college. In this section, we will analyze the specific 3–5 standards under the domains for the Language strand.

The six grade-level standards for Language are organized in the same manner as the domains they are derived from: Conventions of Standard English, Knowledge of Language, and Vocabulary Acquisition and Use. As noted previously, refer to figures 4.1 and 4.2, consider the following questions in your collaborative team:

- What is our current level of knowledge about this standard?

- How can we increase our expertise?

- How will we measure our growth?

Alternatively, you and your team may prefer to use the analysis questions from chapters 2 and 3 (pages 29 and 62). Whichever set of questions you select to guide your discussions, you will be working within a framework that enables you to better understand and implement the CCSS.

Conventions of Standard English

The grade-level standards for this domain speak to the growing command students' gain in the intermediate grades as they apply formal rules of grammar and conventions to their spoken and written communication (see table 4.4, page 118). A challenge with teaching grammar is that the number of rules can quickly overwhelm most learners. Grammar calls for instruction within the context of authentic reading, writing, and

Table 4.4: Language Standards for Domain Conventions of Standard English, Grades 3–5

Anchor Standard	Grade 3 Standards	Grade 4 Standards	Grade 5 Standards
L.CCR.1: Demonstrate command of conventions of standard English grammar and usage when speaking and writing.	**L.3.1:** Demonstrate command of the conventions of standard English grammar and usage when writing or speaking. a. Explain the function of nouns, pronouns, verbs, adjectives, and adverbs in general and their functions in particular sentences. b. Form and use regular and irregular plural nouns. c. Use abstract nouns (like childhood). d. Form and use regular and irregular verbs. e. Form and use the simple verb tenses (for example, I walked; I walk; I will walk). f. Ensure subject-verb and pronoun-antecedent agreement.* g. Form and use comparative and superlative adjectives and adverbs, and choose between them depending on what is to be modified. h. Use coordinating and subordinating conjunctions. i. Produce simple, compound, and complex sentences.	**L.4.1:** Demonstrate command of the conventions of standard English grammar and usage when writing or speaking. a. Use relative pronouns (like who, whose, whom, which, and that) and relative adverbs (where, when, and why). b. Form and use the progressive verb tenses (for example, I was walking; I am walking; I will be walking). c. Use modal auxiliaries (like can, may, and must) to convey various conditions. d. Order adjectives within sentences according to conventional patterns (for example, a small red bag rather than a red small bag). e. Form and use prepositional phrases. f. Produce complete sentences, recognizing and correcting inappropriate fragments and run-ons.* g. Correctly use frequently confused words (like to, too, and two; there and their).*	**L.5.1:** Demonstrate command of the conventions of standard English grammar and usage when writing or speaking. a. Explain the function of conjunctions, prepositions, and interjections in general and their function in particular sentences. b. Form and use the perfect verb tenses (for example, I had walked; I have walked; I will have walked). c. Use verb tense to convey various times, sequences, states, and conditions. d. Recognize and correct inappropriate shifts in verb tense.* e. Use correlative conjunctions (like either/or and neither/nor).

L.CCR.2: Demonstrate command of conventions of standard English capitalization, punctuation, and spelling when writing.	**L.3.2:** Demonstrate command of the conventions of standard English capitalization, punctuation, and spelling when writing.	**L.4.2:** Demonstrate command of the conventions of standard English capitalization, punctuation, and spelling when writing.	**L.5.2:** Demonstrate command of the conventions of standard English capitalization, punctuation, and spelling when writing.
	a. Capitalize appropriate words in titles.	a. Use correct capitalization.	a. Use punctuation to separate items in a series.*
	b. Use commas in addresses.	b. Use commas and quotation marks to mark direct speech and quotations from a text.	b. Use a comma to separate an introductory element from the rest of the sentence.
	c. Use commas and quotation marks in dialogue.	c. Use a comma before a coordinating conjunction in a compound sentence.	c. Use a comma to set off the words yes and no (for example, "Yes, thank you"), to set off a tag question from the rest of the sentence (for example, "It's true, isn't it?"), and to indicate direct address (for example, "Is that you, Steve?").
	d. Form and use possessives.	d. Spell grade-appropriate words correctly, consulting references as needed.	d. Use underlining, quotation marks, or italics to indicate titles of works.
	e. Use conventional spelling for high-frequency and other studied words and for adding suffixes to base words (like sitting, smiled, cries, and happiness).		e. Spell grade-appropriate words correctly, consulting references as needed.
	f. Use spelling patterns and generalizations (like word families, position-based spellings, syllable patterns, ending rules, meaningful word parts) in writing words.		
	g. Consult reference materials, including beginning dictionaries, as needed to check and correct spellings.		

* The Language standards one to three are particularly likely to require continued attention in higher grades as they are applied to increasingly sophisticated writing and speaking.

Source: Adapted from NGA & CCSSO, 2010a, pp. 25 and 28.

speaking demands (Weaver, 1996). Of course, students should be able to identify parts of speech, punctuation, and writing conventions. However, learning fewer but powerful rules deeply is more effective than trying to memorize a bewildering list of rules that are soon forgotten. For example, how many of you know what a correlative conjunction (grade 5) is without looking at examples (such as either/or and neither/nor)? Yet you can all use these correctly while speaking. From an instructional standpoint, identify the most important labels and rules for your students to know, and place a stronger emphasis on teaching grammar and conventions in context.

Generative Writing

One way to teach these essential language skills in context is through generative writing instruction. Teacher-directed instruction offers a valuable opportunity to provide carefully designed lessons that lead students through an organized process for writing with clarity and originality. However, this does not mean that writing should be reduced to isolated skills at the expense of purpose, voice, content, and conventions. We know that problems can occur when a student is full of ideas but does not possess the means to get the message down on paper. Likewise, the student who has mastered the conventions but has difficulty with generating ideas is equally at risk. Through generative writing instruction, teachers provide students with strategies for creating cohesive writing while engaged in authentic tasks. Dorn and Soffos (2001) describe a continuum of difficulty when completing generative writing:

> Adding words to a text is easier to do.
>
> Deleting words from a text is harder to do; deleting lines or phrases is even more difficult.
>
> Substituting words for other words is still more difficult because it requires writers to know multiple meanings for words.
>
> Rearranging sentences and paragraphs is the most difficult skill. (pp. 6–7)

Generative sentences draw the writer's attention to the ways grammar, conventions, and vocabulary work together to convey a message. They are initially brief pieces of text that are systematically expanded under the guidance of the teacher. It is based on Fearn and Farnan's (2001) work with *given word sentences* and can be extended through additional scaffolding. A series of prompts are offered to move students from one idea formulated at the letter or word level to a more fully developed piece of connected text. These prompts are usually paced with a timer to keep the lesson moving and to increase fluency at both the written and creative levels.

A generative sentence session for intermediate-grade writers might begin at the letter level and specify the position within the word. For example, third-grade students are instructed to write a word that contains the letter *c* in the second position. After they have written their words, they share words like *active, icicle, occur,* and *across.* This activity can then precipitate an interesting discussion on why these words all begin with vowels. Once the students have written a word, they now use it in a sentence. The following are sample sentences using the focus words:

- Being *active* is good for your health.
- The *icicle* fell off the roof.
- An accident can *occur* when people are careless.
- I sailed *across* the lake.

In a matter of minutes, students have moved from considering letters and spelling to factoring content and grammar in order to create a sentence that meets the criteria of the English language. Notice how the writer of the third sentence had to figure out where *occur* could fit into the sentence. Stated another way, in a short time the teacher has provided a series of tasks that require the writer to consolidate all the cueing systems to develop an original sentence. It is this consolidation of the visual, structural, and contextual processes that is essential to developing fluent writers.

The activity is not completed until it has been extended to the paragraph level. Students can use the sentence they have created as the topic sentence for a paragraph. Now the challenge is to link a series of ideas together to produce a coherent piece of connected text. In a matter of minutes, students have moved across a continuum of writing skills without ever isolating any of those skills at the expense of meaningful writing.

The number of steps used to get to the paragraph level depends on the developmental level of the writers. Emergent and early writers need letter prompts focused at the beginning and end of words. Transitional and self-extending writers may not need the letter-level prompt at all. A variation of the generative sentence instructional strategy is to begin at the word level. This is especially effective for content area learning because the teacher chooses the focus word. For example, students can be given the word *pilgrim* to construct into accurate sentences. These sentences then serve as a topic sentence for a more detailed informational paragraph that provides the teacher with information about students' content knowledge as well as writing skills.

Spelling

Anchor standard two (L.CCR.2) describes writing conventions, such as punctuation and capitalization, and spelling. The process of encoding in writing parallels decoding development as students gain control of their reading. Expressive language (speaking and writing) development will always lag behind receptive skill levels (listening and reading). You probably notice this with your own literacy as you struggle to spell a word you rarely write, but fully know the meaning and can read it with no difficulty at all.

Researchers have examined the spelling patterns children use, and have named each stage of spelling development: emergent, letter name, within word pattern, syllable juncture, and derivational constancy (Templeton, Johnston, Bear, & Invernizzi, 2008). Although the seeds of spelling knowledge for later derivational constancy are sown early on, most students in grades 3–5 fall into the syllable juncture stage of spelling development.

Emergent Stage

Students at this stage recognize that print conveys a message, but that they are not yet reading. They use scribbles, wavy lines, symbols that resemble letters, and random letters on the page. They often engage in writing-like activities and use drawings as part of their writing. At this stage, there is no correlation between the letter a child writes and the sound it was intended to represent (Johnston, Bear, Invernizzi, & Templeton, 2008).

Letter Name Stage

Students entering this stage have started to master the sound-symbol relationships and the concept of a word. Researchers label this stage based on evidence that students used the names of letters and their emerging understanding of the alphabetic principle to spell (Bear, Invernizzi, Templeton, & Johnston, 2011; Read, 1975). This level of understanding often leads to rather unconventional spelling of words, such as KSL for *castle* and PLES for *police*.

Within Word Pattern Stage

At this stage, students are consolidating their growing knowledge of how combinations of letters can be used to figure out the spelling of unknown ones. Many of the common sight vocabulary words have been mastered and are spelled correctly. Because of their knowledge of letter sounds and short vowel patterns, they can read increasingly difficult texts including chapter books (Bear et al., 2011). Students are no longer relying on individual sounds to spell words, but rather can chunk words and use familiar word families and patterns to make either correct or closer approximations to conventional spelling (Ganske, 2000).

Syllable Juncture

Students at this stage are becoming more skillful readers and writers. They spell most common words correctly and have a growing oral vocabulary. Literacy has increased in value for them as they explore various topics, genres, and ideas. Content areas such as social studies, art, music, science, physical education, and mathematics provide students with access to new information as well as a challenge to read and write in increasingly complex ways. Students at this stage "write to persuade, explain, describe, summarize, and question, using such forms as letters, essays, and various types of response logs to convey their ideas" (Ganske, 2000, p. 17). However, they are now challenged with applying the basic spelling patterns they have learned in the early grades to multisyllabic words they are using in their speech and writing. They still rely on letter sounds and patterns within words, not always to good effect (for example, *confushun* instead of *confusion*). In fact, they are spelling syllable by syllable and facing the question of whether to double or not to double a consonant (for example, *coton* instead of *cotton*). In addition, they are using more compound words, which typically don't require any doubling. Finally, they are learning about how the inflection shifts when a new syllable is introduced (for example, *occur* instead of *reoccur*).

The instructional implications for students at this stage focus on words in which the -*ed* or -*ing* ending requires an *e* to be dropped and the final consonant to be doubled (such as *tapping* and *taping*), doubling the consonant at the syllable juncture (such as *shopping* or *cattle*), and on words with stressed and unstressed syllables (such as *trample* and *hockey*). This is accomplished with teachers' specific instruction on affixes, roots, and bases using sorts (Johnston, Invernizzi, Bear, & Templeton, 2008). Sorts typically feature words or pictures on individual cards. Students use a mat to keep cards organized. There are two kinds of sort cards.

1. **Sound sorts:** These cards build phonemic awareness and feature pictures of common objects possessing the same initial, medial, or final sounds. For example, cards containing pictures of a sun, pan, panda, saw, and pig can be sorted into words that begin with the sound of /s/ and those that begin with the sound of /p/.

2. **Word sorts:** These cards feature printed words instead of pictures.

Students then organize these cards using one of three conditions.

1. **Closed sorts:** Students organize the cards based on stated categories.

2. **Open sorts:** Students examine all the cards to construct their own categories.

3. **Conceptual sorts:** Students categorize cards based on meaning rather than word structure.

Derivational Constancy

This final stage of spelling development typically begins in middle school and continues through adulthood, but the basis for this eventual stage is formed in the intermediate grades. Students at this stage rarely spell the majority of words incorrectly, and they are beginning to learn that words with similar meanings share common spelling patterns (such as *demonstrate*, *demonstration*, and *demonstrable*). Students at this stage learn about this history of the language as well as the etymology (word origins).

The instructional implications for students at this stage allow the teacher to teach students to scrutinize words for their histories. Importantly, the teacher will often learn a lot about words as his or her students engage in this level of word study. Students should be encouraged to keep word journals and to capture the related etymology for the word in these journals. Often students like to record the first known use of the word, related words, and a typical sentence in which the word is used. As Bear et al. (2011) suggest, the teacher can initiate the word study with a simple question, "Did you find any interesting words in your reading?" (p. 20). In addition, Ganske (2000) suggests that teachers focus on silent and sounded consonants (such as *hasten* and *haste*), affixes, and vowel changes (such as *democracy* to *democratic*).

Knowledge of Language

The key word in this domain is *precision*. From grades 3 to 5, students are attending more closely to the way language can be made more precise and concise, especially in understanding how the audience affects punctuation and the addition or subtraction of words and phrases (see table 4.5). In grade 5, students are additionally comparing and contrasting the use of dialects and registers in literature, echoing the core reading standards of craft and structure.

Table 4.5: Language Standards for Domain Knowledge of Language, Grades 3–5

Anchor Standard	Grade 3 Standards	Grade 4 Standards	Grade 5 Standards
L.CCR.3: Apply knowledge of language to understand how language functions in different contexts, to make effective use of choices for meaning or style, and to comprehend more fully when reading or listening.	**L.3.3:** Use knowledge of language and its conventions when writing, speaking, reading, or listening. a. Choose words and phrases for effect.* b. Recognize and observe differences between the conventions of spoken and written standard English.	**L.4.3:** Use knowledge of language and its conventions when writing, speaking, reading, or listening. a. Choose words and phrases to convey ideas precisely.* b. Choose punctuation for effect.* c. Differentiate between contexts that call for formal English (like when presenting ideas) and situations where informal discourse is appropriate (such as in small-group discussion).	**L.5.3:** Use knowledge of language and its conventions when writing, speaking, reading, or listening. a. Expand, combine, and reduce sentences for meaning, reader/listener interest, and style. b. Compare and contrast the varieties of English (like dialects and registers) used in stories, dramas, or poems.

* The skills in Language standards one to three are particularly likely to require continued attention in higher grades as they are applied to increasingly sophisticated writing and speaking.

Source: Adapted from NGA & CCSSO, 2010a, pp. 25 and 29.

Students learn written language by building words into sentences that represent ideas. They also learn to write through taking away what is not necessary. This taking-away process is critical for good editing. A hallmark of effective writing is the way sentences *hang together* to support the reader's understanding of the message the writer is attempting to convey. An effective technique for teaching about the nuances involved in transforming adequate sentences into those that resonate is sentence combining.

Sentence Combining

Sentence combining provides students with an opportunity to utilize syntactic knowledge to create more sophisticated sentences. In a typical activity, students work with a passage of syntactically correct but choppy sentences and rework them to create sentences that preserve the original meaning while increasing the flow of the language.

For example, fifth-grade teacher Carina Sandoval uses an informational selection "The History of Basketball" to teach sentence combining to her students. She selects key sentences from the reading and rewrote them to make them less complex. She then distributes copies of the sentences along with scissors for each of the students to cut out each of the eleven sentence strips. She then challenges them to rewrite the story so that it contains no more than seven sentences. Together they perform *sentence surgery*, cutting unnecessary words out of the disjointed statements. Using the sentence strips as manipulatives, the students move them around on the table until satisfied that they have created a smoother sounding document.

Frederico wrote the new passage using strategies of sentence combining. His passage contains six sentences.

> Basketball has stood the test of time because the rules have barely changed since it was invented. The game was invented by Dr. James Naismith, who was the physical education teacher for a high school. In 1891, the athletic director told him to invent an indoor game to play in the winter because the kids were getting rowdy. Dr. Naismith invented a game in fourteen days with thirteen basic rules. The first game was played with a soccer ball and peach baskets. Dr. Naismith would be considered a genius today, like Bill Gates, but he never made a profit from his invention.

It is important to keep in mind what sentence combining can and cannot do. The effectiveness of sentence combining is diminished in the absence of other components of writing instruction. However, like spoken language, a complex weaving of skills must take place in order to result in a meaningful written message. Syntax is an important part of the fabric of language and these syntactic lessons should be used as one part of a balanced writing program.

Vocabulary Acquisition and Use

The three remaining Language standards are under the domain Vocabulary Acquisition and Use (see table 4.6, page 126). The vocabulary demands on children skyrocket during the school years, ballooning to an estimated 88,500 word families by the time a student is in high school (Nagy & Anderson, 1984). Word families are groups of words related by a common root or pattern, such as *sign*, *significant*, and *signify*. Given the number of word families, it is estimated that students are exposed to over 500,000 words while they are in grades 3 to 9. While these academic language demands are high, it is estimated that everyday speech consists of only 5,000 to 7,000 words (Nagy & Anderson, 1984). Thus, there is a huge difference between the number of words a

Table 4.6: Language Standards for Domain Vocabulary Acquisition and Use, Grades 3–5

Anchor Standard	Grade 3 Standards	Grade 4 Standards	Grade 5 Standards
L.CCR.4: Determine or clarify the meaning of unknown and multiple-meaning words and phrases by using context clues, analyzing meaningful word parts, and consulting general and specialized reference materials, as appropriate.	**L.3.4:** Determine or clarify the meaning of unknown and multiple-meaning word and phrases based on grade 3 reading and content, choosing flexibly from a range of strategies. a. Use sentence-level context as a clue to the meaning of a word or phrase. b. Determine the meaning of the new word formed when a known affix is added to a known word (such as agreeable and disagreeable, comfortable and uncomfortable, care and careless, heat and preheat). c. Use a known root word as a clue to the meaning of an unknown word with the same root (such as company and companion). d. Use glossaries or beginning dictionaries, both print and digital, to determine or clarify the precise meaning of key words and phrases.	**L.4.4:** Determine or clarify the meaning of unknown and multiple-meaning words and phrases based on grade 4 reading and content, choosing flexibly from a range of strategies. a. Use context (such as definitions, examples, or restatements in text) as a clue to the meaning of a word or phrase. b. Use common, grade-appropriate Greek and Latin affixes and roots as clues to the meaning of a word (such as telegraph, photograph, and autograph). c. Consult reference materials (like dictionaries, glossaries, and thesauruses), both print and digital, to find the pronunciation and determine or clarify the precise meaning of key words and phrases.	**L.5.4:** Determine or clarify the meaning of unknown and multiple-meaning words and phrases based on grade 5 reading and content, choosing flexibly from a range of strategies. a. Use context (such as cause and effect relationships and comparisons in text) as a clue to the meaning of a word or phrase. b. Use common, grade-appropriate Greek and Latin affixes and roots as clues to the meaning of a word (such as photograph and photosynthesis). c. Consult reference materials (like dictionaries, glossaries, and thesauruses), both print and digital, to find the pronunciation and determine or clarify the precise meaning of key words and phrases.

L.CCR.5: Demonstrate understanding of figurative language, word relationships, and nuances in meanings.	L.3.5: Demonstrate understanding of word relationships and nuances in word meanings. a. Distinguish the literal and nonliteral meanings of words and phrases in context (like take steps). b. Identify real-life connections between words and their use (for example, describe people who are friendly or helpful). c. Distinguish shades of meaning among related words that describe states of mind or degrees of certainty (for example, knew, believed, suspected, heard, and wondered).	L.4.5: Demonstrate understanding of figurative language, word relationships, and nuances in word meanings. a. Explain the meaning of simple similes and metaphors in context (for example, as pretty as a picture). b. Recognize and explain the meaning of common idioms, adages, and proverbs. c. Demonstrate understanding of words by relating them to their opposites (antonyms) and to words with similar but not identical meanings (synonyms).	L.5.5: Demonstrate understanding of figurative language, word relationships, and nuances in word meanings. a. Interpret figurative language, including similes and metaphors, in context. b. Recognize and explain the meaning of common idioms, adages, and proverbs. c. Use the relationship between particular words (like synonyms, antonyms, and homographs) to better understand each of the words.
L.CCR.6: Acquire and use accurately a range of general academic and domain-specific words and phrases sufficient for reading, writing, speaking, and listening at the college and career readiness level; demonstrate independence in gathering vocabulary knowledge when encountering an unknown term important to comprehension or expression.	L.3.6: Acquire and use accurately grade-appropriate conversational, general academic, and domain-specific words and phrases, including those that signal spatial and temporal relationships (for example, After dinner that night we went looking for them).	L.4.6: Acquire and use accurately grade-appropriate general academic and domain-specific words and phrases, including those that signal precise actions, emotions, or states of being (like quizzed, whined, and stammered) and that are basic to a particular topic (like wildlife, conservation, and endangered when discussing animal preservation).	L.5.6: Acquire and use accurately grade-appropriate general academic and domain-specific words and phrases, including those that signal contrast, addition, and other logical relationships (like however, although, nevertheless, similarly, moreover, and in addition).

Source: Adapted NGA & CCSSO, 2010a, pp. 25 and 29.

student uses commonly as he or she speaks and the number of words needed to be successful in school. This difference in word knowledge is problematic because of its impact on content learning and reading comprehension. In fact, knowledge of vocabulary is a strong predictor of how well a reader will comprehend a text

The fact is that no one could teach 88,500 word families (154 words a day from kindergarten to eighth grade!) nor would it be effective. Fortunately, students acquire many words and phrases through wide reading and experiences. In addition, they need to know how to resolve unknown words outside the company of an adult. Standard four emphasizes teaching students a problem-solving approach using structural and contextual analysis, as well as resources. We refer to this as looking inside a word (structural) and outside a word (context and resources) (Frey & Fisher, 2009).

Looking Inside a Word: Structure

Students use analysis of structural components such as prefixes, suffixes, and root and base words to figure out unfamiliar words that contain familiar morphology. When students understand common prefixes like *re-*, *dis-*, and *un-*, as well as suffixes such as *-s/-es*, *-ing*, and *-er/-or*, they can use this knowledge when they encounter a new word. Word roots are also helpful in understanding the meaning of a new word. For instance, when a student is able to recognize the root in the word *emperor*, he or she can make a good prediction about related words such as *empire* and *imperious*.

Looking Outside a Word: Context

Context clues are the signals authors use to explain a word meaning. There are several types of contextual clues readers use to understand a word, including definitions, synonyms, antonyms, and examples. In the following list, the vocabulary word is underlined and the contextual clue is italicized.

- **Definition:** <u>Philosophy</u> was important to the ancient Greeks. Philosophy means the *beliefs, ideas, and values of the arts and sciences.*

- **Synonym:** The Whiskey <u>Rebellion</u> of 1789 occurred when Western Pennsylvania grain farmers *fought back and protested* a new tax on the alcohol they made from the grain they grew.

- **Antonym:** He came from an <u>impoverished</u> background, unlike his *rich* friend.

- **Example:** <u>Baleen</u> whales don't chew their food like you do because they don't have teeth. Instead, they use a comb-like structure in their mouth called a <u>baleen</u> that *lets the water go in and out, while it keeps the food inside to swallow.*

Looking Outside a Word: Resources

Another way that students figure out unfamiliar words is by using a resource. We don't encourage students to turn to the dictionary first, because we want them to practice their word-solving strategies. We do encourage them to use structural and contextual analysis first, because even if they can't entirely figure out the word's meaning using those two strategies, they at least know something about the word by the time they turn to the resource. Glossaries are especially good, because unlike dictionaries they limit the given meaning to the one used in the related text. In addition, we keep developmental dictionaries in the classroom for students to consult and bookmark online dictionaries. Finally, we stress that asking another peer is also a legitimate resource, which we use frequently ourselves.

Anchor standard five (L.CCR.5) in the domain Vocabulary Acquisition and Use for grades 3–5 details the importance of word relationships in verbal and written language. Relationships between words can be particularly challenging when discussing synonyms. The difference between *annoyance* and *harassment* is a fine but distinct one. This ability to discern between this gradient of meaning is a skill tested on many achievement tests. The difference between the right word and the almost right word can impact the ability of the student to use precise language. These *shades of meaning* can be taught in an imaginative way using paint swatches from the local hardware store (Goodman, 2004). Students attach a paint swatch containing shades of color to notebook paper to illustrate a string of synonyms. Definitions are written to the right of the paint swatch on which the word has been written. For example, third grader Mariana uses a paint swatch with a sea foam color scheme to illustrate shades of meaning and demonstrate the depth of feeling from *happy* to *pleased*, *delighted*, and *overjoyed*.

Another method for teaching students about word relationships is *list-group-label* (Taba, 1967). This instructional technique encourages students to first make predictions about the vocabulary they expect to encounter during a reading then categorize those predictions into an organized frame. By doing this, students will create more detailed predictions. After the reading, they revisit the chart to add information and make corrections. Moss and Loh (2010) advise using the following steps to conduct a successful list-group-label lesson.

1. Select an informational text.

2. Before reading the text, invite students to list vocabulary words they know about the topic of the informational text. Record their ideas on the board.

3. Once the list has been created, discuss how the words and phrased can be grouped.

4. Develop labels for each of the groups they have created. Arrange in a grid and write the words and phrases again under the appropriate categories.

5. Read the text.

6. After the reading, add new words and phrases to the existing categories. New categories can be created as well.

Before reading *And Then What Happened, Paul Revere?* (Fritz, 1996), students in Michael Riley's fourth-grade social studies class make predictions, which are then organized into a chart (see figure 4.4, page 130). After the students read the book, they add other facts to the same chart. The information they add after the reading is in the shaded boxes.

Who Was He?	Where Did He Live?	Why Was He Famous?	How Did He Help the American Revolution?
patriot	A long time ago	He rode a horse.	He told when the British were coming.
colonist	Boston, Massachusetts	There's a poem about him.	He rode to Lexington and Concord to warn minutemen.
silversmith	American colonies	Lanterns in a church told him the message.	
father		He helped the minutemen win the first fight of the war.	

Figure 4.4: Example of list-group-label activity after reading.

Anchor standard six (L.CCR.6), the final one in the domain Vocabulary Acquisition and Use, references grade-appropriate general academic and domain-specific words, providing examples of those that signal temporal relationships in third grade, precise states of being in fourth grade, and logical relationships in fifth. As you have likely already realized, to provide direct instruction for each vocabulary word a student might encounter would be an impossible task. In addition, the appropriate grade-level source words will vary according to materials used, student need, and local context. However, it is essential to have a method for selecting the words that *will* be taught. It is not uncommon for teachers to use a more haphazard approach such as choosing all the *big words* or those that are unusual. However, this is particularly inefficient for ensuring that students are focusing on critical vocabulary. Therefore, we offer the following considerations for choosing vocabulary words to teach.

- **Conceptual value:** Does the word represent an important concept that is needed in order to understanding the reading? For example, *Great Depression* was important for the fifth-grade students in the opening scenario (page 97) to more fully appreciate the hardships Bud faced traveling across America in the 1930s. An important consideration in choosing vocabulary relates to the usefulness of the word. Some words are concepts, while others are labels. Given that students need to acquire a tremendous volume of vocabulary words each year, it seems careless to squander valuable instructional time on words that function only as labels in a particular reading.

  For example, in Lois Lowry's story *The Giver* (1993), a boy is faced with the challenge of confronting truth in his *perfect* community. The word *utopia* is a concept word, for it is central to the understanding of a society with no illness or poverty. On the other hand, the word *tunic* is a label describing the type of clothing the characters wear. *Utopia* is well worth the instructional effort for students to think deeply about the complexities represented by this one word; *tunic* is a word that can be inferred through context clues and is not essential to comprehension. Students also benefit from instruction on the differences between concept and label words because it can prevent them getting bogged down in minutiae at the expense of big ideas. Ms. Pearman's conversation at the beginning of this chapter (page 98) concerning *doggone* illustrates this point.

- **Repeatability:** Is the word going to be used throughout the school year? Some words are worth teaching because they are useful and will be used often. For instance, it is worth taking the time to instruct students on the meaning of *confer* because it will be used throughout the year as students work in small groups with one another.

- **Transportability:** Some words should be selected because they will appear in many subjects or content areas. Teaching students the word *immigration* as it appears in *Letters From Rifka* (Hesse, 1999) is useful because students will also be using this word in social studies.

- **Contextual analysis:** If students can use context clues to determine the word meaning then direct instruction is not necessary. In *The Tale of Despereaux* (DiCamillo, 2009), readers can use context clues to determine both the meaning of *rodent* and the perceptions of the animal in the following sentences: "'Mice are rodents,' said the king. He adjusted his crown. 'They are related to . . . rats. You know our own dark history with rats'" (DiCamillo, 2009, p. 39).

- **Structural analysis:** Words that contain affixes and Latin or Greek root words students are familiar with can be analyzed through structural analysis. For example, the word *magnification* may not need to be included in the list of vocabulary words if students understand the meaning of *magnify* and recognize that the suffix *-tion* is used to change verbs into nouns.

- **Cognitive load:** While there is debate about the number of vocabulary words that teachers should introduce to students at a given time, most agree that the number should reflect the developmental level of the students and the length of the reading (Baumann, 2009; Graves & Watts-Taffe, 2002; Nagy & Scott, 2000; Padak, Bromley, Rasinski, & Newton, 2012). In a brief reading, two to three words is often sufficient for emergent and early readers, while transitional readers can utilize five or so. Most agree that no more than ten should be introduced at any time.

Teachers must create a balance between students learning words in context and learning words through systematic, explicit instruction. Our experience suggests that students will learn a great number of words from well-chosen texts *and* from a thoughtful selection of words for intentional instruction.

Conclusion

The Common Core State Standards for ELA contain several resources that are of value for your collaborative teams to draw on in future activities. The research supports for the standards are located in appendix A of the CCSS (NGA & CCSSO, 2010b). For example, the third-grade team may want to further explore the link between the Speaking and Listening skills and teacher read-alouds. You may recall from chapter 2 on the Reading standards that the text exemplars list read-alouds as a distinct category for third grade (see NGA & CCSSO, 2010c). The section, "Read-Alouds and the Reading-Speaking-Listening Link" in appendix A (NGA & CCSSO, 2010b, p. 27) can initiate further team analysis in identifying both the books to use and the Speaking and Listening activities to accompany them.

Another possible area for collaborative team exploration might include spelling. The section "Reading Foundational Skills" in appendix A of the Common Core ELA includes information on orthography, principles of syllabification, morphology, and derivation (see NGA & CCSSO, 2010b, pp. 17–22). Given that grades 3–5 students are learning to apply these to their reading and writing, the collaborative team may determine that this is a robust area of instruction that can move beyond the conventional program of giving students a list of words on Monday and testing them on Friday.

A third possible path for the collaborative team to follow concerns language grammar and conventions, as well as vocabulary. Again, appendix A (NGA & CCSSO, 2010b) proves a useful resource with a discussion of the relationship of the Conventions of Standard English and Vocabulary Acquisition and Use domains to the Reading, Writing, and Speaking and Listening strands. The description further articulates the integrated nature of language teaching and learning. Additionally, the document offers extensive information on vocabulary and the identification of tier one (everyday-speech), tier two (general-academic), and tier three (domain-specific) words and phrases (see NGA & CCSSO, 2010b, pp. 33–35). The team may decide to identify vocabulary in tier two and tier three that will be taught across the grade band using a schoolwide approach to vocabulary development (Frey & Fisher, 2009).

The Speaking and Listening and Language strands are integral to English language arts, both within the domains of Reading and Writing and across the disciplines. Never again should we tell students that "spelling doesn't count" when in mathematics instruction, or that communication skills don't need instruction because now it's time for social studies. These are foundational to how people learn; all learning is language based. Speaking and listening are used most prominently in the classroom, and the quality of discourse in the classroom is directly related to increased achievement. Jim Britton (1983) says, "Writing floats on a sea of talk" (p. 1), and we fully agree. In fact, we would go one step further: *learning* floats on a sea of talk.

CHAPTER 5

Implementing Formative Assessments to Guide Instruction and Intervention

KEY QUESTIONS

- In your preparations for teaching the lesson, chapter, or unit, to what extent does your collaborative team use the standards and aligned assignments to guide your planning?

- What assessment instruments have you developed collaboratively? Do these instruments accurately reflect the expectations for student achievement that the standards define?

- How do you use your assessment practices to enable students to better understand their learning strengths as well as their needs? In what ways do your assessment activities build students' confidence and motivation?

- To what extent do your schedules provide for timely assessment feedback to students? If changes are needed, how can you go about making them?

- How can you use your assessment data more effectively to modify instruction and help students achieve success?

A week before the school year begins, fourth-grade teacher Hope Collingsworth is gathering assessment data about her new students. She mails each of them a letter with the following message.

> Have you ever wondered how your family came to live in this country? Have you wondered why it's hot in the summer and cold in winter? Welcome back to school! We're going to be studying lots of interesting things this year, and you'll be able to answer these questions and more. A good question starts any learning journey. When you come to school next Monday, be ready to discuss this question: How do we learn?

When her students arrive on the first day of school, Ms. Collingsworth will lead the first discussion of the year on the topic of learning. During this time, she will make notes about her students' speaking and listening skills, one of the first assessments she completes every year. In a few weeks when she knows them better, she will complete a language assessment for each of her students, all of whom are English learners. Like all good teachers, her most powerful assessment tool is her ability to observe her students and make instructional decisions based on her observations.

Ms. Collingsworth views the first six weeks of school as a critical time to establish learning plans for her students. During this period, she will use several surveys to find out more about her students to discern their attitudes toward reading and writing.

"At this age, attitude is everything," she continues, "but I also want to know what they think about themselves as learners. These surveys give me some insight into that." During the first week, she'll administer a series of timed writings to assess their writing fluency and a developmental spelling analysis to establish groups for guided spelling instruction.

The approach she is most excited about is a new one for her this year. "I'm really emphasizing metacognition this year—I want them to know how they know," she says. "That's why I started our school year with the discussion about learning." She will be completing informal reading inventories with her students in order to determine their capacity to read complex narrative and informational and explanatory texts. In fact, the results of this assessment will influence much of her instruction for the year, which will guide her teaching about close reading, critical literacy, and the students' ability to provide evidence from the text to support their claims. "That's the way readers know how they know—by consciously using these techniques to help themselves. Isn't this going to be a great year?"

A Collaborative Planning Team in Action

Ms. Collingsworth's collaborative planning team makes a commitment to fold ongoing assessment into their instructional practices, beginning the first day of school. Initially, team members collect information about each child to establish a baseline for where to begin. These early assessments allow them to group students and get them started with using complex texts, writing for extended periods, and engaging in informal and formal talk. Their instructional units are peppered with formative assessments that make it possible for them to gauge student progress toward goals before the unit has ended. Ms. Collingsworth's team uses the guiding questions at the opening of the chapter (page 133) to shape its assessment plan. Likewise, we encourage you to use these same questions as you identify, design, and analyze the formative and summative assessments you will use in your classrooms.

In the first part of this chapter, we discuss how a formative assessment plan guides instruction. In the latter half of the chapter, we discuss the use of data to guide a response to intervention plan for students who struggle.

The Role of Assessment and the Common Core State Standards

Why do teachers assess students? Think about this for a minute. Is it because they want to find out what students do not know? Or is it because assessments and testing are part of the official behaviors of teachers? Or maybe it's because teachers don't know where to begin instruction without good assessment information. Diane Lapp, Douglas Fisher, James Flood, and Arturo Cabello (2001) suggest that teachers assess students for at least four reasons, including to:

1. Diagnose individual student needs (for example, assessing developmental status, monitoring and communicating student progress, certifying competency, and determining needs)

2. Inform instruction (for example, evaluating instruction, modifying instructional strategies, and identifying instructional needs)

3. Evaluate programs

4. Provide accountability information

As educators, we make numerous decisions about instruction that matter in very significant ways. We believe that these decisions must be based on the assessment information that we gather throughout the learning cycle. This means the teacher doesn't merely march lockstep through the content of a standards-based curriculum, but rather balances the content with the learner needs. These needs are identified through ongoing assessment that is linked to subsequent instruction. In this model, assessment and instruction are considered to be recursive because they repeat as students learn new content. In learner-centered classrooms, teachers first assess to establish what students know and do not know, then plan instruction based on this information. Next, they deliver the instruction they have designed and observe how learners respond. Based on these observations, educators reflect on the results and assess again to determine what needs to be taught next. Figure 5.1 represents this concept.

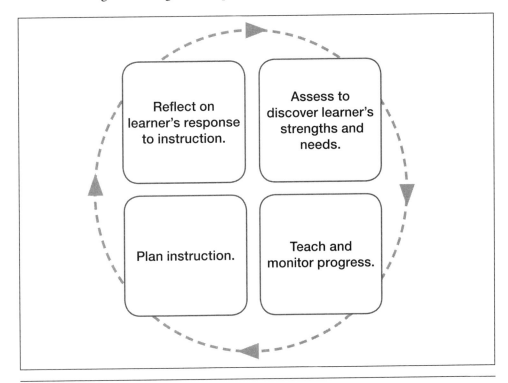

Figure 5.1: Relationship between assessment and instruction.

This model may sound as if it would take a lot of time to complete; in fact, effective teachers perform many of these complex tasks fluidly within the course of their instruction. In well-organized classrooms, assessment happens throughout the day as teachers use questions, discussions, and assignments to measure progress. In addition, teachers administer assessments to monitor progress and formulate future instruction. Assessment equips them with specific information about students who struggle and further informs them about the conditions and content of intervention needed. Teachers are also informed of those students who would benefit from instruction that deepens and enriches their learning. This lies at the very heart of what collaborative planning teams do—they monitor the progress of their students, analyze the results of their teaching, and design intervention supports.

In this chapter, we will concentrate on illustrating assessment events that occur and inform future teaching, so that students can thrive within a Common Core-framed educational system.

Preparing for and responding to large-scale assessments can consume much of the focus and effort of grades 3–5 teachers, elementary school principals, and school district administrators. Implementing the CCSS is unlikely to alter the scrutiny and pressure teachers and administrators face from large-scale assessments.

In 2010, the U.S. Department of Education awarded $330 million in Race to the Top funds to two consortia, representing the majority of states, to develop assessments aligned with the CCSS. (See page 12.) SBAC, representing more than thirty states, received $160 million, PARCC, representing more than twenty-five states, received $176 million. As of this publication, eleven states are members of both consortia (Porter, McMaken, Hwang, & Yang, 2011). Both consortia intend to implement their new state-level common assessments for grades 3–8 and high school during the 2014–2015 school year.

Both assessment consortia aim to design *common* state assessments that are consistent with the vision of the CCSS to include items that assess higher-order thinking, complex texts, writing with evidence, and comparisons across texts. If the assessments take the form their designers intend, then these new state assessments will promote desired instructional changes in favor of an emphasis on deep understanding and reasoning.

Both PARCC and SBAC intend to provide adaptive online tests that will include a mix of constructed-response items, performance-based tasks, and computer-enhanced items that require the application of knowledge and skills. Both assessment consortia are intending to provide summative- and interim-assessment options within the assessment system. You should check your state website for the latest information about progress of the assessment consortia, or visit www.parcconline.org or www.smarterbalanced.org for more information.

For the interim assessments to function as a potential learning tool, teachers will need to ensure they are used for formative purposes—that they are used to provide students and teachers with accurate, timely, fair, and specific information that can move learning forward. This will require that collaborative planning team members are provided time to plan instructional adjustments and that students are supported in relearning content not yet mastered.

However, overreliance on the PARCC and SBAC interim assessments to provide a school district's formative assessment system is not recommended since the effectiveness of this structure to improve student learning is questionable (Popham, 2008). What will make the most difference in terms of student learning is the formative assessment system described later in this chapter. As Wiliam (2007) writes, "If students have left the classroom before teachers have made adjustments to their teaching on the basis of what they have learned about students' achievement, then they are already playing catch-up" (p. 191).

It will be important for team members to become engaged in their state and school's transition to the SBAC or PARCC assessment initiative as part of the full implementation of the Common Core State Standards. The team will need to discuss the following questions:

- How and when will interim assessments be used?

- How will collaborative teams inform families and other members of the school community?

- How will collaborative teams prepare all children in each grade level or school?

Such questions are appropriate as your district- and school-level collaborative teams begin to link state-supported CCSS-related assessments to your implementation of the Common Core State Standards for English language arts. All of this starts with the development and implementation of a formative assessment system. More than formative assessment tools, a *system* allows teachers and teams to systematically evaluate student performance data and make adjustments accordingly. It also allows collaborative teams to identify students in significant need and allocate additional support, often through RTI. A formative assessment system that comes from synthesis of research about the use of student work to inform instruction requires teachers to feed up, feed back, and feed forward.

Feed Up, Back, and Forward

Assessment doesn't begin when the test is passed out; it starts the moment instruction begins. Yet too often assessment is an afterthought, administered mostly to assign a grade. Hattie and Timperley (2007) have an elegant way of describing a model of ongoing assessment: feed up, feed back, and feed forward. We have taken this model a step further to articulate a concrete plan for doing so; one in which we add checking for understanding to the mix (Frey & Fisher, 2011) as a way to feed up by using methods to analyze and assess student understanding. Additionally, we offer a protocol for developing common pacing guides and curricula.

Feed Up by Establishing Purpose

When learners know what is expected of them, what they should be learning, and how they will demonstrate their mastery, their knowledge acquisition is accelerated. This requires clear statements of purpose in order to orient students and make learning intentional. As teachers, we are long accustomed to the practice of defining learning objectives for a lesson: "Students will be able to correctly identify the stages in the life cycle of a frog." But how often are these objectives shared with the people who are supposed to demonstrate them? Establishing purpose means that these intentions are shared with the students, and are used as a guideline for the formative assessment that follows.

We advise further identifying your purpose across three dimensions: (1) content, (2) language, and (3) social purpose. Content is usually the easiest, and the one we often think of first when relating it to objectives. It is the discipline-specific knowledge students should acquire *today*. Learning the stages of a life cycle of a frog is an example of a content purpose. But how will the students demonstrate it? Will they name the stages on a graphic organizer? Will they describe the characteristics of the stages in their collaborative groups using evidence from the text? Will they compare the similarities and differences to another organism that undergoes metamorphosis in a written summary? All of these are related to the language purpose. As we discussed in chapter 4, language is pervasive and includes written and verbal forms, as well as levels of cognition. Finally, a social purpose is useful for grades 3–5 students, who are still developing their ability to learn collaboratively. A social purpose in this lesson might be to provide evidence and examples to help others understand, or to demonstrate listening comprehension by building on the comments of others during a class discussion.

Fifth-grade teacher Emilio Rodriguez uses a feed-up process with every lesson he teaches. "This was a focus of our collaborative team for a while. We developed purpose statements to accompany all of our lessons. Most of us write them on the board so that the students can see them, and it's a good reminder to remember to start off the lesson by making sure they know what we'll be doing and why," he says.

He went on to relay that initially it was a daunting task to do this. "We made the mistake of leaving it up to individual teachers to do, but we quickly realized there was a lot of duplication of effort," he recalls. He also cites the team's key questions (see page 133). "That first question about understanding the student learning targets *in advance of the lesson* was crucial for us. Developing purpose statements together led to lots of good discussion about what we were teaching, and for what purposes."

Checking for Understanding

This is an ongoing process of assessment to determine to what extent students understood the lesson, and to find out what gaps remain. As such, checking for understanding lies at the heart of formative assessment, and it is probably the first thing that comes to mind when teachers think about assessment. There are a variety of methods to check for understanding, including using oral language activities, questions, writing, projects and performances, and tests (Fisher & Frey, 2007a).

Oral Language Activities

When students are doing the talking, the teacher has a chance to assess understanding. A number of classroom structures can be used to provide students an opportunity to talk, including think-pair-share, reciprocal teaching, literacy circles, discussion prompts, and Socratic seminars. For example, as Ms. Ramirez listens to her students discussing a book they are reading as part of their book club, she notices that they are not justifying their responses with evidence from the text. They are skilled at summarizing, but the lack of evidence in their discussions indicates a need to devote additional instructional time to this practice.

In addition to listening as students interact, retellings are a valuable way to check for understanding. Retellings provide the teacher with a glimpse into student thinking. For example, sixth-grade teacher Scott Bradford asks Jasmine to retell a section of a video clip students watched related to glacier formation and movement. As part of her retelling, Jasmine says, "The glaciers take a long time to develop. Well, really they grow like something alive even though they're not alive. They develop when it snows and the snow piles higher and higher. It changes to this special kind of ice, but before that, there is this in-between ice called *firn.*" This retelling lets Mr. Bradford know that much of his teaching has stuck and that Jasmine is well on her way to understanding glaciers.

Questions

Questioning, which can be done orally or in writing, is the most common way teachers check for understanding. Unfortunately, not all questions are worthy of instructional time. To be useful, the initial questions teachers ask should be planned in advance. Of course, additional questions that probe student understanding will come to mind during the interactions teachers have with students, but these initial questions form the expectations for student understanding. Less helpful questions are those we like to call *guess what's in the teacher's head.* More formally known as *initiate-respond-evaluate* or *IRE* (Cazden, 2001), this cycle privileges students who are willing to play the game. For example, when fifth-grade teacher Asep Ali asks, "What is one of the original thirteen colonies?" three or four students raise hands, and Tanya is selected to respond. Tanya says, "New Hampshire," to which the teacher responds, "Good." IRE is typically used with recall information and provides only a few students an opportunity to respond.

Instead, quality checking for understanding suggests that teachers need to ask questions that require more complex and critical thinking and that lots of students need to respond. A number of instructional routines provide students with practice in questioning habits, such as *reciprocal questioning* or *ReQuest* (Manzo, 1969) in which students read with a partner, taking turns asking and answering questions. As they practice, their teacher analyzes the types of questions they are asking and the appropriateness of the answers. Over time (and with instruction and practice) students tire of the literal and recall questions and move toward more interesting questions that require synthesis and evaluation.

Another way to question in an inclusive way is through audience-response systems. These can be as basic as 3 × 5 cards with answers on them that all students hold up to answer a question to as complex as hand-held devices that allow each student to key in a response to a question. As an example, as part of the discussions about *The Raft* (LaMarche, 2002), JoBeth Brent provides her third-grade students with green and red cards, with *Yes* written on the green card and *No* written on the red card. As the teacher reads each statement about the book, students hold up one of their cards to indicate if they agree or disagree. A question about what the story character would find on his trip down the river splits the class, which provides the teacher information about where to focus the lesson next.

Writing

When students are writing, they are thinking. In fact, it's nearly impossible to write and *not* think. That's why short writing-to-learn prompts are so effective for checking for understanding. It's important to develop the prompt so it provides teachers with information about student understanding. For example, the RAFT writing prompt (Santa & Havens, 1995) requires students to consider the role, audience, format, and topic in their writing; this is an excellent way to check for understanding. There are, of course, many other writing prompts that can be used, but RAFT is flexible and teaches perspective. For example, after discussing sportsmanship, Ron Davenport asks his third-grade students to respond to the following RAFT:

R Bronze medal winner

A Gold medal winner

F Greeting card

T Victory

Projects and Performances

On a larger scale, teachers can use projects and performances to check for understanding. Importantly, this should not be done at the end when the project is completed, but rather as students work on these types of activities. A wide range of appropriate projects and performances allow students an opportunity to engage in meaningful work aligned with content standards. As we have noted in chapter 4, the Speaking and Listening standards require that students present, and this category is important for checking for understanding as students learn to demonstrate mastery of these standards. Useful projects and performances range from presentations to group tasks like creating PowerPoint slides.

Tests

Although tests are typically considered a summative assessment tool used for grading and evaluating student performance, they can also be used to check for understanding. Incorrect answers on a test provide teachers with information about what students still need to learn. Tests can be developed in a number of different formats, ranging from multiple-choice to dichotomous choice (true/false, yes/no, agree/disagree) to essays.

Developing Common Pacing Guides and Curricula

Many assessments that are used to check for understanding are designed and implemented by the collaborative planning team in order to gather and analyze data. The Common Core State Standards for English language arts will present a new set of challenges for teachers and administrators. Common assessments, consensus scoring, and item analysis will figure prominently in developing new pacing guides and curricula. You can use the collaborative team meeting record in figure 1.2 (page 10) to do so. The five steps include (Fisher & Frey, 2007a) the following.

1. Construct an initial pacing guide for instruction. Designed to frame the team's work, this guide should be aligned to the expectations in the CCSS.

2. Identify instructional materials such as texts, websites, and media for each unit of study in the pacing guide.

3. Develop common assessments and a schedule for administering them. These should include formative and summative measures and will provide the collaborative team with data to analyze.

4. Engage in consensus scoring and item analysis. These actions serve to determine how students did and to explore the relationship between teaching and learning. It is useful to disaggregate the data to identify trends within and across significant subpopulations. The intent of this process is not to drill down to the individual teacher level, but rather to look across the grade level and grade band to locate patterns. For example, if students with disabilities are making good progress, then what accommodations can this be attributed to? Remember that these data analysis events are also intended for identifying areas of instructional strength, not just locating areas of need.

5. Make revisions to instruction and curriculum and the formation of intervention groups. The outcomes of these team meetings should have dual purposes. The first is to refine instruction for all students in order to improve acquisition of knowledge. In addition, the team needs to examine the circumstances that might be preventing identified students from making sufficient progress. For some students, this may be a matter of reteaching. For those who are displaying a pattern of difficulties that may warrant more formal intervention. Later in this chapter, we will discuss response to intervention as a model for meeting the needs of students who struggle.

Feed Back to Build Student Agency

It would be a mistake to isolate checking for understanding from the feedback loop. Think about the third planning question for a moment: To what degree do our assessment practices build student confidence and encourage them to take responsibility for what they have learned? Students need feedback to guide their learning throughout the process. But not all feedback is useful. The evidence on scoring as feedback suggests that when done in isolation from other types of feedback, such as feedback about processing of the task, it undermines future achievement (Wiliam, 2011). To make feedback more robust, use it judiciously (Hattie & Timperley, 2007). Consider the following forms of feedback.

- **Feedback about the task** (corrective feedback) is effective for alerting a learner to errors. But it is not effective when the student lacks the skills or the knowledge needed to complete the task.

- **Feedback about the processing used in the task** is highly effective because it reminds the learner about his or her cognitive and metacognitive thinking. For example, "I see you're underlining the parts of the story that are important for telling us about the character. That's keeping your ideas organized."

- **Feedback about self-regulation** is also very effective because it assists the learner in self-assessing. For instance, "You were frustrated earlier when your group wasn't listening to your ideas, but you stayed cool and tried again. Did you notice how they listened when you gave them another chance?"

- **Feedback about the person** is considered ineffective because it doesn't provide the learner with any information about what to do next. For example, "Way to go!"

The fourth planning question for the collaborative team is also related to feedback: To what degree do we provide timely formative and summative assessment feedback to students? Even the best feedback will lose its effectiveness if it is not *timely*. In addition, the feedback must be *actionable*; that is, that the learner has a clear sense of direction about what he or she should do next. Additionally, feedback should be *specific* so that the learner is equipped with a necessary level of detail about his or her next actions. Of course, it should be *understandable* in the sense that it should be developmentally and cognitively appropriate for the learner. Taken together, feedback that is well thought out and delivered in a timely fashion will build the agency of the learner and encourage him or her to assume more responsibility for his or her own learning. Because the learner *can*. After all, "Feedback should cause thinking" (Wiliam, 2011, p. 127).

Feed Forward to Inform Instruction

The process of formative assessment is incomplete unless it feeds forward into future instruction. The classroom is the unit of analysis, and the purpose is to locate students who need further instruction *during* (not after) the unit of study. This requires some recordkeeping in order to analyze errors students are making. In our efforts to get to know students as individual learners, we can lose track of patterns that are otherwise right in front of us. Call it the phenomenon of not seeing the forest through the trees, if you will. Error analysis allows us to gain a bit of perspective on who is having difficulty and further prevents us from expending so much effort attending to individual learning problems that we run out of time to instruct everyone.

Error analysis can be accomplished in a number of ways, from a commercially pre-pared checklist to one the teacher makes. This links back to being clear about the pur-pose, and these purpose statements can be used as a platform for clarifying what exactly students should be able to do. By creating a list of specific skills, teachers can not only gather data at the individual level but also look across these checklists to identify groups of students who need further instruction. This may include building background knowl-edge, or simply reteaching. In addition, these teacher-directed small-group arrangements provide the added benefit of having students apply their speaking, listening, and lan-guage skills in the service of content.

Formative and Summative Assessments

The usefulness of every assessment is dependent on a proper fit between purpose and type of assessment used. It is important to remember that every assessment is useful and not useful *at the same time*. Any given assessment is useful in the hands of a conscien-tious educator who understands the limitations of the tool being used. Any given assess-ment is useless if it is interpreted to show something it was not intended to show. You would be very suspicious of a doctor who ordered a chest x-ray when you were seeking help for a sprained ankle. There is nothing inherently wrong with a chest x-ray, but it is simply the wrong test for the task. In the same regard, the type of reading or writing assessment selected must match its intended use. Guillaume (2004) offers these consid-erations for selecting an assessment. Each assessment needs to be:

- Tied to your stance on learning
- Driven by learning goals
- Systematic
- Tied to instruction
- Connected to the learner
- Integrated into a manageable system

Tied to Your Stance on Learning

Every teacher brings a philosophy of education and a view of literacy to his or her practice. It is important to recognize how assessment choices fit into that perspective. For example, an educator who possesses a viewpoint of learning as a developmental phenomenon will be interested in assessment instruments that reflect benchmarks of developmental phases of learning. Teachers with a skills-based orientation will find skills measures to be useful.

Driven by Learning Goals

Classroom assessments should be consistent with the expectations of the grade-level Common Core State Standards. The standards are outcome-based and articulate the *what* of learning. As educators, we make the decisions about *how* we get there.

Systematic

Teachers select assessments that can be administered and analyzed in a systematic way at both the individual and class levels. Good assessments should possess data recording and analysis protocols that make it easy for the teacher to interpret the information at a later date. In addition, the teacher must determine how often they will be administered. Finally, each assessment should measure what it purports to measure (valid) and yield results that are consistent across administrations and assessors (reliable).

Tied to Instruction

Although this seems apparent, it is worth stating again. Assessment should be linked directly to instruction, either to determine what should be taught next (pretesting) or to check for understanding of skills or strategies that have just been taught (post-testing). Assessments that are not connected to instruction are likely to be frustrating for students because they appear purposeless and inadequate for teachers because they do not provide relevant information.

Connected to the Learner

Assessments are intended to be completed in conjunction with the learners' needs. They should be designed to capture the work of children in the act of learning. Whether through listening to a student reading text (as is the case with running records and informal reading inventories) or using a rubric to discuss a student's writing (analytic writing assessment), these tools are intended to involve the learner in their own measures of progress.

Integrated Into a Manageable System

No teacher can devote all his or her time to collecting and analyzing assessment data. The demands of assessment on the time available can become overwhelming and even crowd equally valuable instructional time. Therefore, it is in the teacher's interest to understand what each assessment does, then select the one that best fits the needs of the students, teacher, and curriculum. The collaborative planning team is the ideal forum for selecting and designing formative assessments that inform instruction.

One of the challenges teachers and teams often encounter with feed-forward systems is creating a manageable system. When teachers evaluate students' work, they often provide individual students with feedback. As we have discussed, this is helpful for the student, and perhaps his or her parents, in understanding areas of strength and need. But it is less helpful for teachers in terms of determining what to teach next. Frankly, it's hard for any of us to remember the range of errors and misconceptions that students have and then to organize instruction around those instructional needs. To effectively implement a formative assessment system, teachers and their collaborative teams need to regularly examine student work and identify patterns in the strengths and needs identified in the data.

For example, fourth-grade teacher Claire Richards and her collaborative team developed an error-analysis tool based on their efforts to teach correct verb-form usage to use in the beginning of the year to determine students' skills and needs (see figure 5.2). They use this tool to analyze student's writing to determine areas of strength and need. The challenge is to figure out what to do with the information once it has been collected. Without some analysis of the patterns that emerge in each classroom, teachers will have a hard time teaching students based on need and are at risk of teaching the whole class content that some students have already mastered.

Verb Form	Total Attempts	Correct Usage	Errors	Percentage of Errors
Student's writing displays subject-verb agreement.				
Student uses the simple present tense.				
Student uses simple past tense with -ed.				
Student uses simple future tense with the helping verb will.				
Student uses the present perfect tense with the helping verbs has and have.				
Student uses the past perfect tense with the helping verb had.				
Student demonstrates the ability to write to be verbs is, am, are, was, and were with singular and plural nouns.				

Source: Adapted from D. Rilling, personal communication, 2012. Used with permission.

Figure 5.2: Error analysis for fourth-grade verb usage.

Visit **go.solution-tree.com/commoncore** for a reproducible version of this figure.

We recommend that collaborative teams develop an error-analysis system that includes all student information on a single sheet of paper. In this case, rather than have the columns for total attempts, correct usage, errors, and percentage of errors, teachers list student initials for those students who have not yet met the standard on any indicator (see figure 5.3).

Verb Form	Students With No Errors	Students With One to Three Errors	Students With Four or More Errors
Student's writing displays subject-verb agreement.			
Student uses the simple present tense.			
Student uses simple past tense with -ed.			
Student uses simple future tense with the helping verb will.			
Student uses the present perfect tense with the helping verbs has and have.			
Student uses the past perfect tense with the helping verb had.			
Student demonstrates the ability to write to be verbs is, am, are, was, and were with singular and plural nouns.			

Figure 5.3: Revised error analysis for fourth-grade verb usage for students not meeting learning target.

Visit **go.solution-tree.com/commoncore** for a reproducible version of this figure.

In one classroom, there were three students who made excessive errors in subject-verb agreement, a Common Core State Standard that is monitored throughout elementary school. These students need additional instruction, probably small-group instruction, to meet this standard, but the rest of the class does not.

If there are specific students who fail to respond to quality core instruction, including the re-teaching that comes from careful analysis of student work, the teacher should present this situation and the data that have been collected to the collaborative team for consideration. The team may recommend that an RTI committee evaluate each student, as will be discussed in the next section. Or the team may decide that the student needs to receive some additional instruction from the classroom teacher or from another team member. The key here is to realize that no teacher is alone in this process. Students fail to respond to quality instruction for a whole host of reasons and when teams of teachers get together to problem solve these situations, students' benefit. Unfortunately, in some schools, asking other teachers for assistance or advice is seen as a weakness. If we are to implement the Common Core State Standards well, we are going to have to talk with our colleagues much more often. Furthermore, we are going to have to talk with them about students who struggle, despite our best efforts to ensure their success.

What to Do When Students Struggle

Sometimes the assessment information that is collected will indicate that a student, or group of students, has failed to make progress. Sometimes this happens because the student did not receive adequate quality core instruction, perhaps due to absences or a specific teaching situation. In that case, the student needs to be retaught the content using evidence-based practices that ensure success. Sometimes students fail to make progress despite really good core instruction. In this case, the student likely needs some sort of supplemental or intensive intervention. RTI is a system to respond when students fail to progress. As with other efforts to implement the Common Core State Standards, RTI requires the mobilization of collaborative teams and entire school systems (Buffum et al., 2009).

Although RTI has become more broadly known through its inclusion in the Individuals With Disabilities Education Improvement Act of 2004 (http://idea.ed.gov), response to intervention has existed as a theory and practice for decades. As described in federal legislation, the intent is twofold: (1) to provide early intervention for students who are struggling and (2) to allow for an alternate means of identifying the presence of a learning disability. Unfortunately, in some schools the latter purpose has overshadowed the former. In an effort to establish a balance between the two, a growing number of states are investing in a response to instruction and intervention (RTI^2) model. Before focusing on the major components of an RTI model, we will explore five mistakes that are commonly made when school systems attempt to establish and implement an RTI^2 program.

Mistake One: Thinking Intervention, Not Instruction

An effective RTI effort begins with a quality core program—this is the first tier of the widely known three-tier model of RTI (for more information, visit the RTI Action Network at www.rtinetwork.org). A quality core program includes the kind of scaffolded learning experiences expressed through a gradual release of responsibility instructional framework (Frey & Fisher, 2010). This framework includes establishing the purpose of the lesson for students, modeling one's cognitive processes by thinking aloud, and providing guided instruction through the use of questions, prompts, and cues. In addition, students spend much of their time learning collaboratively with their peers in productive group work, before attempting independent learning. Without these practices firmly in place in all classrooms, the supplemental and intensive intervention efforts of any school will be quickly overwhelmed by students who are failing simply because they are not receiving quality core instruction.

Consider the practices of fifth-grade teacher Tina Pham who skillfully weaves these instructional practices throughout a lesson on the original thirteen colonies. She starts with a clear purpose, namely that students will learn the names and locations of each of the thirteen colonies. As part of the lesson, she modeled her thinking about the locations of each of the colonies using a large map projected via a document camera.

She tells her students, "I like to start at the top of the map because I remember this one [*pointing*] is New Hampshire. And then I remember that the one with a little hook is Massachusetts. Then I have to think a little bit because I used to confuse Rhode Island and Connecticut. The way I remember it now is alphabetical. *C* comes before *R*, so this one [*pointing*] is Connecticut and this one [*pointing*] is Rhode Island. Then the big one behind them is easy, that's New York. I remember that because most of the land of New York does not touch the sea, just a tiny little bit."

She continues, talking about each of the colonies and their physical characteristics. She then invites students to develop a mnemonic in their groups to remember the thirteen colonies.

As she says, "It's only thirteen, and you can probably remember them, but I know that talking about the names with other people and developing a mnemonic together will really help you remember them. When we're done with our mnemonics, we'll share them and then read more of the social studies text. As we read, we'll know the location that the author is talking about because we can visualize the location in our minds."

As groups of students get to work, Ms. Pham meets with students who have experienced difficulty, as shown in the error-analysis data, this far in the unit for additional guided instruction. They leave their group when she calls them to have a discussion with her. At one point, she meets with three students who have difficultly locating the colonies on a map of North America.

"Let's take another look at the map of North America," Ms. Pham says. "We've looked at this map before, but let's make sure that we know the area we're talking about before we look at a different version of the map of North America. Can you all point to the area where the thirteen colonies are? Nice job, team. Samara, tell me how you knew that."

Samara replies, "I know that they are on the side by the water; the water is on the right side."

"Yeah," Adrianna says, "that's different from the side we live on. We have water on the left side."

"Are there other features that you remember?" Ms. Pham asks. "I'm wondering, because sometimes maps are shown from a different angle or perspective."

Andi responds, "I remember that it is curved like this." She draws a concave shape with her hand. "There are parts that stick out on the top and bottom."

"Oh, yeah," Samara remembers, "like that part right here on the bottom. Native Americans lived there too, but not the colony people."

"You're right, Ms. Pham says. "Native Americans lived all through these parts [*pointing to the East Coast*], and the colonists also lived here [*pointing to the area of the thirteen colonies*]. So, let's look at a different map and see if we can't find the thirteen colonies on this version. Then, we can find the exact colonies."

As they work with their teacher, these three students are developing an increased understanding of the content such that they have sufficient background knowledge to read the textbook. The other students in the classroom are creating mnemonics that they will share with the class and with the three students who participated in guided instruction with their teacher. If these three students do not make progress, their teacher will discuss them with her collaborative team and the team may recommend that they receive Tier 2 or Tier 3 interventions. At this point, however, their needs are being met through formative assessments that provide Ms. Pham with information about their instructional needs.

Mistake Two: Relying on Prepackaged Curricula

While commercial programs labeled as being intervention friendly can provide some needed practice materials, they cannot replace well-designed and individualized lessons targeting the specific needs of students who require intervention. Fourth-grade teacher Allen Rittenhouse accesses the resources of Elena Vargas, a reading specialist who provides supplemental and intensive interventions.

As Mr. Rittenhouse notes, "I know that my students receive support that they need to learn the content of fourth grade. This includes some basic skills, but also the content that our class is studying. If we just bought a program, it would probably not help with all of the specific informational texts that I use in the class for science and social studies." Shannon, a student in Mr. Rittenhouse's fourth-grade classroom, is fortunate to attend a school that has avoided the error of relying exclusively on commercial programs for intervention.

"We used to drag all the Tier 2 students through the same reading program, regardless of their needs," says Ms. Vargas. "Now I align my materials with what students are using in their classrooms."

Shannon, who struggles with reading comprehension, reads passages from her textbooks and other related texts.

"I know from talking with Mr. Rittenhouse that Shannon's class is studying the planets right now, so the vocabulary and reading work that we're doing together right now is about the solar system," says Ms. Vargas. She counts on regular communication with the other teachers to design lessons that are meaningful.

Mistake Three: Isolating Teachers and Interventionists

Coordinating learning across the school day is challenging under the best of circumstances, and adding intervention efforts to the mix can be difficult. It can be tempting to simply put one teacher in charge of an RTI program, give him or her a classroom, and turn attention to other matters. But isolating interventionists from classroom teachers severely limits the kind of collaboration Ms. Vargas and Mr. Rittenhouse are able to accomplish for Shannon's benefit. Instead, consider the team effort each student in an RTI² program will need to be successful. It is important to make sure that every student receiving supplemental or intensive interventions has an identified person coordinating instruction, and another coordinating intervention. Communication between these two educators can bridge the divide that can otherwise occur when interventions are disconnected from the core curriculum.

Mistake Four: Making Data Decisions Alone

Ms. Vargas, Shannon's intervention teacher, collects data each time she meets with the student so that she can track progress and determine what is working. Importantly, data collection and analysis also reveal when something is not working. "I initially started out with using timed writing with Shannon, but I quickly discovered that wasn't the best approach. I found that when I gave her a chance to discuss the reading with me for a few minutes first, her writing improved in length and content," says Ms. Vargas.

Both Mr. Rittenhouse and Ms. Vargas serve on the school's RTI² subcommittee, an outgrowth of the Student Study Team formed to closely examine the circumstances surrounding specific students' behavioral or academic difficulties. The subcommittee meets regularly to discuss the progress of students receiving intervention supports. Ms. Vargas brings her data to the group for discussion and finds that others can sometimes spot a trend she had overlooked. In addition, she can share her insights about what she has found effective. For instance, she recommended that Mr. Rittenhouse and Shannon's other teachers have the students plan their writing orally in advance of extended writing assignments. "I've been more conscious of doing this for the last few weeks," Mr. Rittenhouse observes, "and I'm seeing that it's giving her a chance to organize her thoughts better. Her reports of information are beginning to improve."

Mistake Five: Leaving the Family Out of the Planning

Family involvement is key when students who struggle are participating in RTI² efforts. In fact, the family may possess quite a bit of information that can be helpful in determining ways to accelerate student learning. As keepers of their child's history, family members have firsthand knowledge about what has worked in the past. However, this information can come too late in the process when families are contacted only after a student's lack of response to intervention warrants a referral for special education testing. It is understandable that families can become justifiably frustrated when they learn that their child has been involved in an intervention for months without their knowledge.

At Shannon's school, her father and stepmother initially met with the administrator who oversees the RTI[2] program. She explains why their daughter was being recommended for supplemental intervention and gathered information from them about past efforts. Ms. Vargas speaks with them on the phone each month to share Shannon's progress and ask them about their observations. While Shannon's eventual progress means that she didn't require a referral for special education testing, the school gains two important allies. "I was caught a little off guard when the school called me," Shannon's father says. "After all, she'd only been there for a few weeks." The girl's stepmother continues, "But we really got to see how much the school cares about Shannon's progress. It's good to know she's not just an anonymous student at a busy school."

Assessment, Intervention, and Instruction

Fourth-grade teacher Natalie Thompson regularly collects formative assessment information for all of her students in order to ensure they are receiving appropriate instruction. She tracks her observations and keeps a record of formal assessment results. She often uses her conferring time during independent activities as a time to collect and record further individual assessment information. One student has been worrying her. Steven is an English learner identified as gifted and talented. However, he has various needs in oral language, reading, and writing as he continues to learn the English language. She further describes Steven as extremely shy. "I need to help him open up, make friends, and feel more comfortable taking risks." Some of this is due to his status as an English learner. He is at the intermediate stage of language development. "I always need to keep in mind that I have to compare English learners to true peers, and not let his chronological age alone be the only metric I use," she says.

Steven knows how to use his resources when he is stuck, which is a major strength as students approach middle school. He uses the teacher's assistance as his last resort to finding an answer to a question, and he is highly motivated and maintains a positive attitude in the classroom. His peers respect him and welcome him into social groups in the classroom. Although he has many strengths and positive aspects, Steven has needs related to his language development and vocabulary. Because his English proficiency is at the intermediate stage, Steven needs specific help in order to improve his language development. He also needs help in reading and writing. He uses the resources Ms. Thompson has created with him such as personal dictionaries, the word wall, and other resources based on a particular lesson or unit of study. But despite a good attitude and some additional supports as a language learner, his progress has stalled. Ms. Thompson decides that the first place to begin is with some individual assessments.

Assessment

Ms. Thompson began by revisiting the assessments she already had done with Steven. For example, she administered an informal reading inventory at the beginning of the school year. In addition, she had the state language assessment for English learners. The results suggested that Steven needs to focus on vocabulary and writing.

Ms. Thompson continued by collecting a timed writing sample and used both a holistic rubric and an analytic writing tool to gain a more detailed view of his on-demand writing. From her analysis of this data, she also noted that he still needs help with spelling, paragraph development, and vocabulary enhancement. It was also clear that Steven has complex thoughts, but has difficulty communicating exactly what he wants to say.

She also data collected informally during focus lessons and guided reading sessions using an error-analysis protocol her collaborative team had developed for small-group discussions. For example, Ms. Thompson noted that during guided reading, Steven read quietly and was somewhat reserved. He chose to participate, but rarely contributed to the discussion. When Ms. Thompson used a retelling inventory, she wrote that Steven could identify some of the main ideas, but could not provide many story details. He was also unable to use evidence from the text, even when prompted.

Ms. Thompson also remarks that examining a student's homework or independent practice component of a lesson is a great way to see if a student understands the material. She says, "Homework is a wonderful assessment tool because the students are required to apply previously taught information. It's not the stuff they are currently learning. But it's content they learned earlier this school year, or even last year. If students can apply learned concepts to an independent homework assignment in a different environment in which they learned it, they have mastered the concepts." When she reviewed Steven's homework, she found that while he tried to complete most of these assignments, few of them were done accurately.

Intervention

Based on her findings, Ms. Thompson took the data she had analyzed to her next collaborative planning team meeting. She described Steven's lack of progress in some areas and offered evidence of his strengths as well. The team provided reflective feedback and invited her to speculate about possible solutions. The discussion proved to be a moment of clarity for her. "He's an English learner, and some of his difficulties might be explained by that. But it's his lack of progress since the beginning of this year that's so troublesome. It's time to move into some Tier 2 supplemental instruction."

Ms. Thompson is bilingual herself but knew she could draw on other resources. She consulted with the school's bilingual specialist, Ruth Montoya, to design supplemental instruction for Steven. Together they made a plan for daily additional small-group instruction with two other students. "I wanted to make sure there were other people he had to talk to," Ms. Thompson says. The daily lesson format began with a making words activity. Based on her assessment information, Ms. Thompson knew that Steven sometimes had trouble with correctly identifying letter clusters, which greatly impacted his spelling. Her anecdotal notes indicate that Steven "was pretty successful at this activity because he found the pattern in the word families. Steven found the letter/sound patterns almost immediately while some students struggled making the words correctly."

Instruction

She monitored his progress by using a developmental spelling inventory. Because Steven caught on rapidly, Ms. Thompson altered her objectives for this supplemental intervention after several weeks and focused on transferring his learning to writing in content areas. "I didn't stop with having him make words and sort them," she says. "But I found what worked and I shifted those activities to his Tier 1 guided instruction." Ms. Montoya looked at the results of the teacher's progress-monitoring data and agreed.

An ongoing area of focus was Steven's oral language development. Ms. Thompson knew that her students, including Steven, loved games and competition with their classmates. She also knew that he needed to increase his knowledge of words and their meanings. As a result, she modified the game Pictionary to emphasize general academic vocabulary. She noted that when it was Steven's turn to draw a picture, he felt no hesitation because he wanted to win for his teammates. When his teammates drew pictures, Steven was actively participating and using his oral language skills to participate in the game. Steven left all his previous insecurities aside for this game because he was so engaged.

Because Steven also needed writing instruction, Ms. Thompson decided to make this the focus of her conferring time. She created a lesson using a children's thesaurus to increase Steven's vocabulary to *five-dollar words*—longer, technical words—rather than just *dollar words*—common, everyday words. The use of the thesaurus was helpful for Steven when the students were writing cinquain poems about their week of school that was held at the art museum. Her analysis of his poems revealed that rather than using simple words like he did in his haikus from earlier in the year, Steven was now using more complex vocabulary in his cinquains because he looked up the words he wanted to use in a thesaurus to find other words that meant the same thing.

Steven received Tier 2 supplemental intervention for several months. The goal wasn't to rapidly eliminate any traces of the learning progression of someone still learning a new language. Rather, Ms. Thompson was alarmed that his learning had slowed and needed more time with him to figure out what could work. "He didn't need Tier 2 supplemental intervention because I was worried about him having a disability," she remarks. "I knew he needed more instruction, and I needed to be more effective than I was. Really, it was a win-win situation for both of us."

Conclusion

To really operationalize the information in this chapter, collaborative teams in professional learning communities must develop their assessment literacy (Boudett, City, & Murname, 2005). In other words, they need to know which assessment tools work for which tasks and in which ways. Furthermore, teams in collaboration with site leadership should develop an assessment calendar so that all members of the school community know which assessments they should give, and when. Once the more formal assessment system has been developed, then the team can turn its attention to monitoring student progress. This occurs on many levels, ranging from the analysis of state assessments to reviews of student work. Regardless of the level, the collaborative planning team should be on the lookout for students who are not responding to quality core instruction. In these cases, the team needs to discuss ways to ensure that students are supported, including through informal reteaching and formal response to intervention systems. Highly effective teams have data management systems for keeping track of students as they progress through the year and early warning systems that provide alerts when students are not making progress.

This chapter has focused on the many kinds of assessment instruments available to classroom teachers in order to plan instruction, monitor growth, and evaluate learning. However, as we stated previously, no one assessment is ideal for every situation. As the teacher, you will need to determine what kinds of information you need about your students, which instruments can give you the information you are seeking, and how much time you have available to administer and analyze. Therefore, we believe that the assessments themselves need to be analyzed to see which best fit your purposes. Every time you consider a new assessment, we encourage you to ask yourself the following questions.

- **"What does this assessment really measure?"** Don't let the title of the assessment fool you. Look closely at the task demands to make sure that other skills like reading, writing, or using language ability don't confound results.

- **"What will the results tell me? What will the results *not* tell me?"** Make sure that the information an assessment yields is necessary and is not duplicated by another assessment. Also, be clear about what other assessments you might need to administer in order to give a more complete picture of a learner.

- **"What expenditure of my time and effort will be required to administer and analyze the assessment?"** The time you have available is finite. Some assessments are time consuming to administer but yield rich results that make them worthwhile. Others are quick but may deliver little in the way of useable information. Plan your assessment calendar like you do your curricular one to ensure you are using your time (and that of your students) wisely.

- **"How will this assessment help my instruction?"** A New Zealand proverb says, "You don't fatten sheep by weighing them." We are concerned about the increase in the amount of testing that is occurring in schools in the name of accountability. Instructional time is increasingly being whittled away in order to do more testing. In this chapter, we have focused on classroom assessments that translate to instructional decisions. When chosen wisely and analyzed with care, these assessments ultimately save instructional time by allowing you to be more precise in choosing what to teach, what to reteach, and when the student can move on to new content.

- **"How can this assessment figure into my intervention efforts and reporting requirements?"** Not every assessment is suitable for such determinations, as some are diagnostic and others are used for accountability. However, the majority of assessments should provide information about next steps instruction and the possible need for intervention. In addition, these assessments should help inform the team about the effectiveness of the intervention efforts, known as *progress monitoring*, and can also be helpful in parent and student conferences as well as reporting successes and needs on report cards.

The Common Core State Standards for English language arts present an opportunity for teachers and their teams to collaborate in ways that result in improved student achievement. These standards represent a shift as well as an increase in expectations, and our students deserve nothing less than our very best effort to ensure that they meet these standards so they are prepared for the next stage in their life, middle school, high school, and beyond.

REFERENCES AND RESOURCES

Abbott, R. D., Berninger, V. M., & Fayol, M. (2010). Longitudinal relationships of levels of language in writing between grades 1 and 7. *Journal of Educational Psychology, 102*(2), 281–298.

Adler, M. J., & Van Doren, C. (1972). *How to read a book.* New York: Touchstone. (Original work published 1940)

Afflerbach, P., Pearson, P. D., & Paris, S. (2008). Clarifying differences between reading skills and reading strategies. *The Reading Teacher, 61*(5), 364–373.

Aliki. (1986). *A medieval feast.* New York: HarperCollins.

Allington, R. L. (2002). You can't learn much from books you can't read. *Educational Leadership, 60*(3), 16–19.

Alvermann, D. E. (1991). The discussion web: A graphic aid for learning across the curriculum. *The Reading Teacher, 45*, 92–99.

American Speech-Language-Hearing Association. (2012). *What is language? What is speech?* Accessed at www.asha.org/public/speech/development/language_speech.htm on May 11, 2012.

Baum, L. F. (2000). *The wonderful wizard of Oz.* New York: HarperCollins.

Baumann, J. F., Font, G., Edwards, E. C., & Boland, E. (2005). Strategies for teaching middle-grade students to use word-part and context clues to expand reading vocabulary. In E. H. Hiebert & M. L. Kamil (Eds.), *Teaching and learning vocabulary: Bringing research to practice* (pp. 179–205). Mahwah, NJ: Erlbaum.

Baumann, J. (2009). Vocabulary and reading comprehension. In S. E. Israel & G. G. Duffy (Eds.), *Handbook of research on reading comprehension* (pp. 323–346). New York: Routledge.

Bayliss, V. A. (1994). Fluency in children's writing. *Reading Horizons, 34*, 247–256.

Bayliss, V. A., & Walker, N. L. (1990). *Bayliss/Walker scales: Holistic writing evaluation, grades 1–6.* Springfield: Southwest Missouri State University.

Bear, D. R., Invernizzi, M. R., Templeton, S., & Johnston, F. R. (2011). *Words their way: Word study for phonics, vocabulary, and spelling instruction* (5th ed.). Boston: Allyn & Bacon.

Beck, I. L., McKeown, M. G., & Kucan, L. (2002). *Bringing words to life: Robust vocabulary instruction.* New York: Guilford Press.

Beck, I. L., McKeown, M. G., & Kucan, L. (2008). *Creating robust vocabulary: Frequently asked questions and extended examples.* New York: Guilford Press.

Beers, S. F., & Nagy, W. E. (2011). Writing development in four genres from grades three to seven: Syntactic complexity and genre differentiation. *Reading & Writing Quarterly, 24*, 183–202.

Bereiter, C., & Scardamalia, M. (1987). *The psychology of written composition.* Hillsdale, NJ: Erlbaum.

Berninger, V. M., & Abbott, R. D. (2010). Listening comprehension, oral expression, reading comprehension, and written expression: Related yet unique language systems in grades 1, 3, 5, and 7. *Journal of Educational Psychology, 102*(3), 635–651.

Birenbaum, M., Kimron, H., & Shilton, H. (2011). Nested contexts that shape assessment for learning: School-based professional learning community and classroom culture. *Studies in Educational Evaluation, 37*(1), 35–48.

Blachowicz, C. L. Z., & Fisher, P. (2002). *Teaching vocabulary in all classrooms* (2nd ed.). Upper Saddle River, NJ: Merrill/Prentice Hall.

Blake, W. (1971). The ecchoing green. In *Songs of innocence* (p. 42). New York: Dover. (Original work published 1789)

Bossert, T. S., & Schwantes, F. M. (1996). Children's comprehension monitoring: Training children to use rereading to aid comprehension. *Reading Research and Instruction, 35*, 109–121.

Boudett, K. P., City, E. A., & Murname, R. J. (Eds.). (2005). *Data wise: A step-by-step guide to using assessment results to improve teaching and learning.* Cambridge, MA: Harvard University Press.

Bransford, J. D., Brown, A. L., & Cocking, R. R. (Eds). (2000). *How people learn: Brain, mind, experience, and school.* Washington, DC: National Academy Press.

Britton, J. (1983). Writing and the story of the world. In B. Kroll & E. Wells (Eds.), *Explorations in the development of writing theory, research, and practice* (pp. 3–30). New York: Wiley.

Buffum, A., Mattos, M., & Weber, C. (2009). *Pyramid response to intervention: RTI, professional learning communities, and how to respond when kids don't learn.* Bloomington, IN: Solution Tree Press.

Bullough, R. V., Jr., & Baugh, S. C. (2008). Building professional learning communities within a university–public school partnership. *Theory Into Practice, 47*(4), 286–293.

Burnford, S. (1997). *The incredible journey.* New York: Yearling.

California Department of Education. (n.d.). *Common Core State Standards: Frequently asked questions.* Sacramento, CA: Author. Accessed at www.cde.ca.gov/re/cc/ccssfaqs2010.asp on August 31, 2012.

Callison, D., & Preddy, L. (2006). *The blue book on information age inquiry, instruction, and literacy.* Santa Barbara, CA: Libraries Unlimited.

Cazden, C. B. (2001). *Classroom discourse: The language of teaching and learning.* Portsmouth, NH: Heinemann.

Chall, J. S., Conard, S., & Harris, S. (1977). *An analysis of textbooks in relation to declining SAT scores.* Princeton, NJ: College Entrance Examination Board.

Chall, J. S., & Jacobs, V. A. (2003). Poor children's fourth-grade slump. *American Educator, 27*(1), 14–15; 44.

Chetty, R., Friedman, J. N., & Rockoff, J. E. (2011). *The long-term impacts of teachers: Teacher value-added and student outcomes in adulthood* (Executive summary of National Bureau of Economic Research working paper no. 17699). Accessed at http://obs.rc.fas.harvard.edu/chetty/value_added.html on May 11, 2012.

Coker, D. (2007). Writing instruction for young children. In S. Graham, C. A. MacArthur, & J. Fitzgerald (Eds.), *Best practices in writing instruction* (pp. 101–118). New York: Guilford Press.

Council of Chief State School Officers. (2012). *The Common Core State Standards: Supporting districts and teachers with text complexity.* Webinar delivered January 26, 2012. Washington, DC: Author. Accessed at https://ccsso.webex.com/mw0306ld/mywebex/default.do;jsessionid=KGR NPd6hnnshndyz9QLk5qthTtFvV6yPkQTTPg2XGvZ489Lm2pTQ!1006560109?nomenu=tru e&siteurl=ccsso&service=6&rnd=0.8424170944354614&main_url=https%3A%2F%2Fccsso .webex.com%2Fec0605ld%2Feventcenter%2Fprogram%2FprogramDetail.do%3FtheAction %3Ddetail%26siteurl%3Dccsso%26cProgViewID%3D22 on February 10, 2012.

Cox, B. E., Shanahan, T., & Tinzmann, M. B. (1991). Children's knowledge of organization, cohesion, and voice in written exposition. *Research in the Teaching of English, 25*(2), 179–218.

Crain, W. (2000). *Theories of development: Concepts and applications* (4th ed.). Upper Saddle River, NJ: Prentice Hall.

Csikszentmihalyi, M. (1997). *Finding flow: The psychology of engagement with everyday life.* New York: Basic Books.

Csikszentmihalyi, M. (2000). *Beyond boredom and anxiety: Experiencing flow in work and play.* San Francisco: Jossey-Bass.

Curtis, C. P. (1999). *Bud, not Buddy.* New York: Delacorte.

D'Aluisio, F., & Menzel, P. (2008). *What the world eats.* New York: Random House.

Daniels, H. (2002). *Literature circles: Voice and choice in book clubs and reading groups.* Portland, ME: Stenhouse.

Darling-Hammond, L. (2010). *The flat world and education: How America's commitment to equity will determine our future.* New York: Teachers College Press.

Davidson, C. N. (2011). *Now you see it: How the brain science of attention will transform the way we live, work, and learn.* New York: Viking.

DiCamillo, K. (2000). *Because of Winn-Dixie.* Cambridge, MA: Candlewick Press.

DiCamillo, K. (2009). *The tale of Despereaux: Being the story of a mouse, a princess, some soup, and a spool of thread.* Cambridge, MA: Candlewick Press.

Dorn, L. J., & Soffos, C. (2001). *Scaffolding young writers: A writers' workshop approach.* Portland, ME: Stenhouse.

DuFour, R., DuFour, R., & Eaker, R. (2008). *Revisiting professional learning communities at work: New insights for improving schools.* Bloomington, IN: Solution Tree Press.

DuFour, R., DuFour, R., Eaker, R., & Many, T. (2010). *Learning by doing: A handbook for professional learning communities at work™* (2nd ed.). Bloomington, IN: Solution Tree Press.

DuFour, R., & Marzano, R. J. (2011). *Leaders of learning: How district, school, and classroom leaders improve student achievement.* Bloomington, IN: Solution Tree Press.

Duke, N. K., & Roberts, K. M. (2010). The genre-specific nature of reading comprehension. In D. Wyse, R. Andrews, & J. Hoffman (Eds.), *The Routledge international handbook of English, language and literacy teaching* (pp. 74–86). London: Routledge.

Eaker, R., DuFour, R., & DuFour, R. (2002). *Getting started: Reculturing schools to become professional learning communities.* Bloomington, IN: Solution Tree Press.

Elbow, P. (1981). *Writing with power: Techniques for mastering the writing process.* New York: Oxford University Press.

Faber, J. E., Morris, J. D., & Lieberman, M. G. (2000). The effect of note taking on ninth grade students' comprehension. *Reading Psychology, 21*, 257–270.

Farley, W. (2008). *The black stallion.* New York: Random House. (Original work published 1941)

Fearn, L., & Farnan, N. (2001). *Interactions: Teaching writing and the language arts.* Boston: Houghton Mifflin.

Feldman, E. B. (1999). *They fought for freedom: Children in the civil rights movement.* New York: McGraw-Hill.

Ferris, H. (Ed.). (1957). The new colossus. In *Favorite poems, old and new, selected for boys and girls* (p. 448). New York: Doubleday. (Original work published 1883)

Fisher, D., & Frey, N. (2007a). *Checking for understanding: Formative assessment techniques for your classroom.* Alexandria, VA: Association for Supervision and Curriculum Development.

Fisher, D., & Frey, N. (2007b). *Scaffolded writing instruction: A gradual release model.* New York: Scholastic.

Fisher, D., & Frey, N. (2010). *Enhancing RTI: How to ensure success with effective classroom instruction and intervention.* Alexandria, VA: Association for Supervision and Curriculum Development.

Fisher, D., Frey, N., & Rothenberg, C. (2011). *Response to intervention for English learners.* Bloomington, IN: Solution Tree Press.

Fisher, D., Frey, N., & Lapp, D. (2012). *Text complexity: Raising rigor in reading.* Newark, DE: International Reading Association.

Fitzhugh, L. (1964). *Harriet the spy.* New York: Leaf.

Fleischman, P. (1988). Fireflies. In *Joyful noise: Poems for two voices* (pp. 11–14). New York: HarperCollins.

Fleischman, P. (1996). *Dateline: Troy.* Cambridge, MA: Candlewick Press.

Frey, N., & Fisher, D. (2007). *Reading for information in elementary school: Content literacy strategies to build comprehension.* Upper Saddle River, NJ: Merrill Prentice Hall.

Frey, N., & Fisher, D. (2008). *Teaching visual literacy: Using comic books, graphic novels, anime, cartoons and more to develop comprehension and thinking skills.* Thousand Oaks, CA: Corwin Press.

Frey, N., & Fisher, D. (2009). *Learning words inside and out: Vocabulary instruction that boosts achievement in all subject areas.* Portsmouth, NH: Heinemann.

Frey, N., & Fisher, D. (2010). Getting to quality: A meeting of the minds. *Principal Leadership, 11*(1), 68–70.

Frey, N., & Fisher, D. (2011). *The formative assessment action plan: Practical steps to more successful teaching and learning.* Alexandria, VA: Association for Supervision and Curriculum Development.

Frey, N., Fisher, D., & Berkin, A. (2008). *Good habits, great readers: Building the literacy community.* Upper Saddle River, NJ: Allyn & Bacon.

Frey, N., Fisher, D., & Everlove, S. (2009). *Productive group work: How to engage students, build teamwork, and promote understanding.* Alexandria, VA: Association for Supervision and Curriculum Development.

Frey, N., Fisher, D., & Gonzalez, A. (2010). *Literacy 2.0: Reading and writing in the 21st century.* Bloomington, IN: Solution Tree Press.

Frey, N., Fisher, D., & Nelson, J. (2010). Lessons scooped from the melting pot: California district increases achievement through English language development. *Journal of Staff Development, 31*(5), 24–28.

Fritz, J. (1996). *And then what happened, Paul Revere?* New York: Puffin Books.

Gamoran, A. (2007). *Standards-based reform and the poverty gap: Lessons from No Child Left Behind.* Brookings Institution.

Ganske, K. (2000). *Word journeys: Assessment-guided phonics, spelling, and vocabulary instruction.* New York: Guilford Press.

Ganske, L. (1981). Note-taking: A significant and integral part of learning environments. *Educational Communication and Technology: A Journal of Theory, Research, and Development, 29,* 155–175.

Gentry, J. R. (2006). *Breaking the code: The new science of beginning reading and writing*. Portsmouth, NH: Heinemann.

Gibbons, G. (1995). *Planet Earth/Inside out*. New York: Morrow.

Gilbert, J., & Graham, S. (2010). Teaching writing to elementary students in grades 4–6: A national survey. *Elementary School Journal, 110*(4), 494–518.

Gilbreth, F. B., & Carey, E. G. (2002). *Cheaper by the dozen*. New York: Harper Perennial.

Goodman, L. (2004). Shades of meaning: Relating and expanding word knowledge. In G. E. Tompkins & C. Blanchfield (Eds.), *Teaching vocabulary: 50 creative strategies, grades K–12* (pp. 85–87). Upper Saddle River, NJ: Merrill/Prentice Hall.

Graves, M. F., & Watts-Taffe, S. M. (2002). The place of word consciousness in a research-based vocabulary program. In A. E. Farstrup & S. J. Samuels (Eds.), *What research has to say about reading instruction* (3rd ed.; pp. 140–165). Newark, DE: International Reading Association.

Guillaume, A. M. (2004). *K-12 classroom teaching: A primer for new professionals* (2nd ed.). Upper Saddle River, NJ: Pearson.

Hattie, J., & Timperley, H. (2007). The power of feedback. *Review of Educational Research, 77*, 81–112.

Hayes, D. P., Wolfer, L. T., & Wolfe, M. (1996). Schoolbook simplification and its relation to the decline in SAT-Verbal scores. *American Educational Research Journal, 33*, 489–508.

Hesse, K. (1999). *Letters from Rifka*. New York: Scholastic.

Horney, M. A., Anderson-Inman, L., Terrazas-Arellanes, F., Schulte, W., Mundorf, J., Wiseman, S., et al. (2009). Exploring the effects of digital note taking on student comprehension of science texts. *Journal of Special Education Technology, 24*(3), 45–61.

Individuals With Disabilities Education Act, 20 U.S.C. § 1400 (2004).

Individuals With Disabilities Education Improvement Act of 2004, Pub. L. No. 108–446, 118 Stat. 2647.

Jeong, J., Gaffney, J. S., & Choi, J. (2010). Availability and use of informational texts in second-, third-, and fourth-grade classrooms. *Research in the Teaching of English, 44*(4), 435–456.

Johnston, F. R., Bear, D. R., Invernizzi, M. R., & Templeton, S. (2008). *Words their way: Word sorts for letter name-alphabetic spellers* (2nd ed.). Upper Saddle River, NJ: Prentice Hall.

Johnston, F. R., Invernizzi, M. R., Bear, D. R., & Templeton, S. (2008). *Words their way sorts for syllable and affix spellers* (2nd ed.). Upper Saddle River, NJ: Prentice Hall.

Jones, C. F. (1991). *Mistakes that worked: 40 familiar inventions and how they came to be*. New York: Doubleday,

Joyce, B., & Showers, B. (1983). *Power in staff development through research on training*. Washington, DC: Association for Supervision and Curriculum Development.

Kanold, T., Briars, D., & Fennell, F. (2012). *What principals need to know about teaching and learning mathematics*. Bloomington, IN: Solution Tree Press.

Kasper-Ferguson, S., & Moxley, R. (2002). Developing a writing package with student graphing of fluency. *Education and Treatment of Children, 25*, 249–267.

King, G., Headington, T., Scorsese, M., Depp, J. (Producers), & Scorsese, M. (Director). (2011). *Hugo* [Motion picture]. United States: Paramount Pictures.

Kinniburgh, L., & Shaw, E. (2007). Building reading fluency in elementary science through readers' theatre. *Science Activities, 44*(1), 16–22.

Kress, G. (1999). Genre and the changing contexts for English language arts. *Language Arts, 76*(6), 461–469.

LaMarche, J. (2002). *The raft*. New York: HarperCollins.

Langer, J. (1986). *Children reading and writing: Structures and strategies*. Norwood, NJ: Ablex.

Lapp, D., Fisher, D., Flood, J., & Cabello, A. (2001). An integrated approach to the teaching and assessment of language arts. In S. R. Hurley & J. V. Tinajero (Eds.), *Literacy assessment of second language learners* (pp. 1–26). Needham Heights, MA: Allyn & Bacon.

Larson, K. (2006). *Hattie big sky*. New York: Random House.

Lathem, E. C. (Ed.). (1979). Stopping by woods on a snowy evening. In *The poetry of Robert Frost: The collected poems, complete and unabridged*. New York: Henry Holt. (Original work published 1923)

Leithwood, K., McAdie, P., Bascia, N. & Rodrigue, A. (Eds.). (2006). *Teaching for deep understanding: What every educator should know*. Thousand Oaks, CA: Corwin Press.

Lennon, C., & Burdick, H. (2004). *The Lexile framework as an approach for reading measurement and success. A white paper from the Lexile framework for reading*. Accessed at www.lexile.com /m/uploads/whitepapers/Lexile-Reading-Measurement-and-Success-0504_MetaMetrics Whitepaper.pdf on July 23, 2012.

Lezotte, L.W. (1991). *Correlates of effective schools: The first and second generation*. Okemos, MI: Effective Schools Products.

Littleton, E. B. (1998). Emerging cognitive skills for writing: Sensitivity to audience in five- through nine-year-olds' speech. *Cognition and Instruction, 16*(4), 399–430.

Lowry, L. (1993). *The giver*. Boston: Houghton Mifflin.

MacLachlan, P. (1985). *Sarah, plain and tall*. New York: HarperCollins.

Manak, J. (2011). The social construction of intertextuality and literary understanding: The impact of interactive read-alouds on the writing of third graders during writing workshop. *Reading Research Quarterly, 46*(4), 309–311.

Manzo, A. (1969). ReQuest: A method for improving reading comprehension through reciprocal questioning. *Journal of Reading, 12*, 123–126.

Martinez, M., Roser, N., & Strecker, S. (1999). "I never thought I could be a star": A readers theatre ticket to fluency. *The Reading Teacher, 52*(4), 326–334.

May, L. (2011). Animating talk and texts: Culturally relevant teacher read-alouds of informational texts. *Journal of Literacy Research, 43*(1), 3–38.

McCutchen, D., Covill, A., Hoyne, S. H., & Mildes, K. (1994). Individual differences in writing: Implications of translating fluency. *Journal of Educational Psychology, 86*, 256–266.

McNeill, K. L. (2011). Elementary students' views of explanation, argumentation, and evidence, and their abilities to construct arguments over the school year. *Journal of Research in Science Teaching, 48*(7), 793–823.

Michaels, S., O'Connor, C., & Resnick, L. (2008). Deliberative discourse idealized and realized: Accountable Talk in the classroom and in civic life. *Studies in Philosophy and Education, 27*(4), 283–297.

Miller, C. (1984). Genre as social action. *Quarterly Journal of Speech, 70*, 151–167.

Moore, N., & MacArthur, C. (2012). The effects of being a reader and of observing readers on fifth-grade students' argumentative writing and revising. *Reading & Writing, 25*(6), 1449–1478.

Montgomery, S. (2006). *Quest for the tree kangaroo: An expedition to the Cloud Forest of New Guinea*. Orlando: Houghton Mifflin.

Moss, B. (2003). *Exploring the literature of fact: Children's nonfiction trade books in the elementary classroom*. New York: Guilford Press.

Moss, B. (2004). Teaching expository text structures through informational trade book retellings. *The Reading Teacher, 57*, 710–179.

Moss, B. (2005). Making a case and a place for effective content area literacy instruction in the elementary grades. *The Reading Teacher, 59*(1), 46–55.

Moss, B., & Loh, V. (2010). *35 strategies for guiding readers through informational texts.* New York: Guilford Press.

Mueller, A., & Fleming, T. (2001). Cooperative learning: Listening to how children work at school. *Journal of Educational Research, 94*, 259–265.

Muschla, G. R. (1993). *Writing workshop survival kit.* Paramus, NJ: The Center for Applied Research in Education.

Nagin, C. (2003). *Because writing matters: Improving student writing in our schools.* San Francisco: Jossey-Bass.

Nagy, W. E., & Anderson, R. C. (1984). How many words are there in printed school English? *Reading Research Quarterly, 19*, 303–330.

Nagy, W. E., & Scott, J. A. (2000). Vocabulary processes. In M. L. Kamil, P. B. Mosenthal, P. D. Pearson, & R. Barr (Eds.), *Handbook of reading research* (vol. 3; pp. 269–284). Mahwah, NJ: Erlbaum.

National Educational Goals Panel. (1998). *Ready schools.* Washington, DC: Author.

National Governors Association Center for Best Practices & Council of Chief State School Officers. (2010a). *Common core state standards for English language arts & literacy in history/social studies, science, and technical subjects.* Washington, DC: Author. Accessed at www.corestandards.org /assets/CCSSI_ELA%20Standards.pdf on February 10, 2012.

National Governors Association Center for Best Practices & Council of Chief State School Officers. (2010b). *Common core state standards for English language arts & literacy in history/social studies, science, and technical subjects. Appendix A: Research supporting key elements of the standards.* Washington, DC: Author. Accessed at www.corestandards.org/assets/Appendix_A.pdf on February 10, 2012.

National Governors Association Center for Best Practices & Council of Chief State School Officers. (2010c). *Common core state standards for English language arts & literacy in history/social studies, science, and technical subjects. Appendix B: Text exemplars and sample performance tasks.* Washington, DC: Author. Accessed at www .corestandards.org/assets/Appendix_B.pdf on February 10, 2012.

National Governors Association Center for Best Practices & Council of Chief State School Officers. (2010d). *Common core state standards for English language arts & literacy in history/social studies, science, and technical subjects. Appendix C:Samples of student writing.* Washington, DC: Author. Accessed at www.corestandards.org/assets /Appendix_C.pdf on February 10, 2012.

National Governors Association Center for Best Practices & Council of Chief State School Officers. (2010e). Common core state standards for mathematics. Washington, DC: Authors. Accessed at www.corestandards.org/assets/CCSSI_Math%20Standards.pdf on November 22, 2010.

National Institute of Child Health and Human Development. (2000). *Report of the National Reading Panel. Teaching children to read: An evidence-based assessment of the scientific research literature on reading and its implications for reading instruction* (NIH Publication No. 00-4769). Washington, DC: U.S. Government Printing Office.

National Research Council. (1996). *National science education standards.* Washington, DC: National Academies Press.

Nelson, K. (2008). *We are the ship: The story of the negro baseball leagues.* New York: Hyperion.

Otfinoski, S. (1996). *The kid's guide to money: Earning it, saving it, spending it, growing it, sharing it.* New York: Scholastic.

Padak, N., Bromley, K., Rasinski, T., & Newton, E. (2012). Vocabulary: Five common misconceptions. *Educational Leadership Online, 69.* Accessed at www.ascd.org/publications/educational -leadership/jun12/vol69/num09/Vocabulary@-Five-Common-Misconceptions.aspx on July 25, 2012.

Paris, S. G. (2005). Reinterpreting the development of reading skills. *Reading Research Quarterly, 40*(2), 184–202.

Pauk, W. (1974). *How to study in college.* Boston: Houghton Mifflin.

Pearson, P. D., & Gallagher, M. (1983). The instruction of reading comprehension. *Contemporary Educational Psychology, 8,* 317–344.

Pianta, R. C., Belsky, J., Houts, R., & Morrison, F. (2007). Opportunities to learn in America's elementary classrooms. *Science, 315,* 1795–1796.

Poe, E. A. (1844/1988). *Marginalia.* Charlottesville: University of Virginia Press.

Popham, W. J. (2008). *Transformative assessment.* Alexandria, VA: Association for Supervision and Curriculum Development.

Porter, A., McMaken, J., Hwang, J., & Yang, R. (2011). Common core standards: The new U.S. intended curriculum. *Educational Researcher, 40*(3), 103–116.

Purcell-Gates, V., Duke, N. K., & Martineau, J. A. (2007). Learning to read and write genre-specific text: Roles of authentic experience and explicit teaching. *Reading Research Quarterly, 42,* 8–45.

Raphael, T. E. (1986). Teaching question-answer relationships, revisited. *The Reading Teacher, 39,* 198–205.

Rappaport, D. (2008). *Lady Liberty: A biography.* Cambridge, MA: Candlewick Press.

Rasinski, T. (2011). The art and science of teaching reading fluency. In D. Lapp & D. Fisher (Eds.), *Handbook of research in teaching the English language arts* (3rd ed.; pp. 238–246). New York: Routledge.

Read, C. (1975). *Children's categorization of speech sounds in English.* Urbana, IL: National Council of Teachers of English.

Richards, I. A. (1929). *Practical criticism.* London: Cambridge University Press.

Sacramento County Office of Education. (2012). *California's Common Core State Standards for English language arts, literacy in history/social studies, science, and technical subjects.* Sacramento, CA: Author. Accessed at www.scoe.net/castandards/agenda/2010/ela_ccs_recommendations.pdf on August 31, 2012.

Salahu-Din, D., Persky, H., & Miller, J. (2008). *The nation's report card: Writing 2007.* Washington, DC: U.S. Department of Education, Institute for Educational Sciences.

Santa, C. M., & Havens, L. T. (1995). *Project CRISS: Creating independence through student-owned strategies.* Dubuque, IA: Kendall/Hunt.

Schmar-Dobler, E. (2003). Reading on the Internet: The link between literacy and technology. *Journal of Adolescent & Adult Literacy, 47,* 80–85.

Selznick, B. (2007). *The invention of Hugo Cabret.* New York: Scholastic.

Short, K., Schroeder, J., Kauffman, G., & Kaser, S. (2004). Thoughts from the editors. *Language Arts, 81*(3), 183.

Simmons, J. (2003). Responders are taught not born. *Journal of Adolescent and Adult Literacy, 48,* 684–693.

Smith, D. J. (2002). *If the world were a village: A book about the world's people*. Tonawanda, NY: Kids Can Press.

Stanley, D. (1999). *Raising sweetness*. New York: Putnam.

Stevens, R. J., & Slavin, R. E. (1995). Effects of a cooperative learning approach in reading and writing on academically handicapped and nonhandicapped students. *Elementary School Journal, 95*, 241–262.

Sticht, T. G., & James, J. H. (1984). Listening and reading. In P. D. Pearson, R. Barr, M. L. Kamil, & P. Mosenthal (Eds.), *Handbook of reading research* (Vol. 1; pp. 293–317). White Plains, NY: Longman.

Stoll, L., Bolam, R., McMahon, A., Wallace, M., & Thomas, S. (2006). Professional learning communities: A review of the literature. *Journal of Educational Change, 7*(4), 221–258.

Taba, H. (1967). *Teacher's handbook for elementary social studies*. Reading, MA: Addison-Wesley.

Templeton, S. Johnston, F. R., Bear, D. R., & Invernizzi, M. R. (2008). *Words their way: Word sorts for derivational relations spellers* (2nd ed.). Upper Saddle River, NJ: Prentice Hall.

Toulmin, S. (1958). *The uses of argument*. Cambridge, UK: Cambridge University Press.

Troia, G. A., & Graham, S. (2002). The effectiveness of a highly explicit, teacher-directed strategy instruction routine: Changing the writing performance of students with learning disabilities. *Journal of Learning Disabilities, 35*, 290–305.

Turbill, J., & Bean, W. (2006). *Writing instruction K–6: Understanding process, purpose, audience*. Katonah, NY: Owen.

Vanneman, S. (2011). Note taking as easy as . . . ABC LOU. *School Library Monthly, 27*(4), 23–25.

Vygotsky, L. S. (1978). *Mind in society: The development of higher psychological processes*. Cambridge, MA: Harvard University Press.

Weaver, C. (1996). *Teaching grammar in context*. Portsmouth, NH: Heinemann.

Wheeler, R. (2006). *Code-switching: Teaching standard English in urban classrooms*. Urbana, IL: National Council of Teachers of English.

White, E. B. (2001). *Charlotte's web*. New York: HarperCollins. (Original work published 1952)

Wilder, L. I. (2010). *Little house on the prairie*. New York: HarperCollins.

Wiliam, D. (2007). Content then process: Teacher learning communities in the service of formative assessment. In D. Reeves (Ed.), *Ahead of the curve: The power of assessment to transform teaching and learning* (pp. 183–204). Bloomington, IN: Solution Tree Press.

Wiliam, D. (2011). *Embedded formative assessment*. Bloomington, IN: Solution Tree Press.

Wood, D. (1998). *How children think and learn* (2nd ed.). Oxford, UK: Blackwell.

Yovanoff, P., Duesbery, L., & Alonzo, J. (2005). Grade-level invariance of a theoretical causal structure predicting reading comprehension with vocabulary and oral language fluency. *Educational Measurement: Issues & Practices, 24*(3), 4–12.

INDEX

A

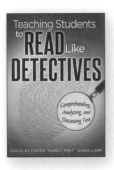

Teaching Students to Read Like Detectives
Douglas Fisher, Nancy Frey, and Diane Lapp

Prompt students to become the sophisticated readers, writers, and thinkers they need to be to achieve higher learning. Explore the important relationship between text, learner, and learning, and gain an array of methods to establish critical literacy in a discussion-based and reflective classroom.
BKF499

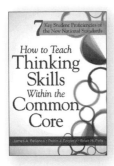

How to Teach Thinking Skills Within the Common Core
James A. Bellanca, Robin J. Fogarty, and Brian M. Pete

Empower your students to thrive across the curriculum. Packed with examples and tools, this practical guide prepares teachers across all grade levels and content areas to teach the most critical cognitive skills from the Common Core State Standards.
BKF576

Collaborative Teacher Literacy Teams, K–6
Elaine K. McEwan-Adkins

Explore the work of collaborative literacy teams from their formation to the employment of successful student-focused strategies. Find professional growth units in each chapter that provide educators with the opportunity to discuss key concepts, self-reflect, and remain focused on student achievement.
BKF491

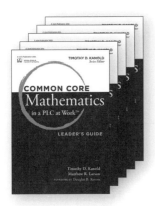

Common Core Mathematics in a PLC at Work™ Series
Edited by Timothy D. Kanold

These teacher guides illustrate how to sustain successful implementation of the Common Core State Standards for Mathematics. Discover what students should learn and how they should learn it at each grade level. Comprehensive and research-affirmed analysis tools and strategies will help you and your collaborative team develop and assess student demonstrations of deep conceptual understanding *and* procedural fluency.
Joint Publications With the National Council of Teachers of Mathematics
BKF566, BKF568, BKF574, BKF561, BKF559

Solution Tree | Press

a division of
Solution Tree

Visit solution-tree.com or call 800.733.6786 to order.

Solution Tree

Solution Tree's mission is to advance the work of our authors. By working with the best researchers and educators worldwide, we strive to be the premier provider of innovative publishing, in-demand events, and inspired professional development designed to transform education to ensure that all students learn.

The mission of the International Reading Association is to promote reading by continuously advancing the quality of literacy instruction and research worldwide.